W9-AAT-296

Jane Lynch

by Cherese Cartlidge

LUCENT BOOKS
A part of Gale, Cengage Learning

GALE
CENGAGE Learning·

Detroit • New York • San Francisco • New Haven, Conn • Waterville, Maine • London

GALE
CENGAGE Learning·

LIBRARY OF CONGRESS CATALOGING-IN-PUBLICATION DATA

Cartlidge, Cherese.
  Jane Lynch / by Cherese Cartlidge.
    pages cm. -- (People in the news)
  Summary: "This series profiles the lives and careers of some of today's most prominent newsmakers. Whether covering contributions and achievements or notorious deeds, books in this series examine why these well-known personages garnered public attention"-- Provided by publisher.
  Includes bibliographical references and index.
  ISBN 978-1-4205-0887-1 (hardback)
  1. Lynch, Jane, 1960---Juvenile literature. 2. Actors--United States--Biography--Juvenile literature. I. Title.
  PN2287.L95C37 2013
  792.02'8092--dc23
  [B]
                                                      2013033967

Lucent Books
27500 Drake Rd.
Farmington Hills, MI 48331

ISBN-13: 978-1-4205-0887-1
ISBN-10: 1-4205-0887-3

Contents

Fame and celebrity are alluring. People are drawn to those who walk in fame's spotlight, whether they are known for great accomplishments or for notorious deeds. The lives of the famous pique public interest and attract attention, perhaps because their experiences seem in some ways so different from, yet in other ways so similar to, our own.

Newspapers, magazines, and television regularly capitalize on this fascination with celebrity by running profiles of famous people. For example, television programs such as *Entertainment Tonight* devote all their programming to stories about entertainment and entertainers. Magazines such as People fill their pages with stories of the private lives of famous people. Even newspapers, newsmagazines, and television news frequently delve into the lives of well-known personalities. Despite the number of articles and programs, few provide more than a superficial glimpse at their subjects.

Lucent's People in the News series offers young readers a deeper look into the lives of today's newsmakers, the influences that have shaped them, and the impact they have had in their fields of endeavor and on other people's lives. The subjects of the series hail from many disciplines and walks of life. They include authors, musicians, athletes, political leaders, entertainers, entrepreneurs, and others who have made a mark on modern life and who, in many cases, will continue to do so for years to come.

These biographies are more than factual chronicles. Each book emphasizes the contributions, accomplishments, or deeds that have brought fame or notoriety to the individual and shows how that person has influenced modern life. Authors portray their subjects in a realistic, unsentimental light. For example, Bill Gates—cofounder of the software giant Microsoft—has been instrumental in making personal computers the most vital tool of the modern age. Few dispute his business savvy, his perseverance, or his technical expertise, yet critics say he is ruthless in his dealings with competitors and driven more by his desire to maintain Microsoft's dominance in the computer industry than by an interest in furthering technology.

In these books, young readers will encounter inspiring stories about real people who achieved success despite enormous obstacles. Oprah Winfrey—one of the most powerful, most watched, and wealthiest women in television history—spent the first six years of her life in the care of her grandparents while her unwed mother sought work and a better life elsewhere. Her adolescence was colored by pregnancy at age fourteen, rape, and sexual abuse.

Each author documents and supports his or her work with an array of primary and secondary source quotations taken from diaries, letters, speeches, and interviews. All quotes are footnoted to show readers exactly how and where biographers derive their information and provide guidance for further research. The quotations enliven the text by giving readers eyewitness views of the life and accomplishments of each person covered in the People in the News series.

In addition, each book in the series includes photographs, annotated bibliographies, timelines, and comprehensive indexes. For both the casual reader and the student researcher, the People in the News series offers insight into the lives of today's newsmakers—people who shape the way we live, work, and play in the modern age.

Jane's World

Jane Lynch, who plays the bizarre and oftentimes caustic cheerleading coach Sue Sylvester on the hit TV show *Glee*, is one of the most well-known women on TV today. She has made a name for herself playing cocky, straight-shooting characters with a wry sense of humor. She is also known for taking on roles that were originally written for men; in fact, she was cast as a man in a play on more than one occasion. Today she has found a niche for herself playing strong female characters, both on TV and in films.

An Offbeat Sense of Humor

A big part of Lynch's success is her wry sense of humor. In person, Lynch is candid, honest, and very direct—much like many of her characters. She also has a great sense of humor. "I love trying to find what's funny about everything,"[1] she says. Her sense of humor is oftentimes self-deprecating, and she seems to delight in putting herself down in a humorous way. For example, at the unveiling ceremony for her wax statue in 2010, Lynch thanked Madame Tussauds wax museum in Hollywood by gushing, "This is amazing! Oh, you guys are great—and I think you might have minimized my [butt], and I appreciate that."[2]

Lynch's offbeat, wicked sense of humor was also evident at the 2011 Golden Globe Awards ceremony, when she took the stage to accept the award for best supporting performance in a series. During her acceptance speech, she smiled disarmingly and proclaimed, "I am nothing if not falsely humble."[3] The British newspaper *Guardian* calls Lynch "one of the most beloved scene-stealers" around today and adds that she is "one of those rare comic actors who doesn't need to say things that are funny to get a laugh—she can make anything funny."[4]

An "Unfeminine Woman"

Lynch is not only funny; she is a trailblazer, the rare woman who has succeeded in taking on the male world. When she hosted the 63rd Primetime Emmy Awards in September 2011, she became only the third solo female host in the show's history. (The other two were Angela Lansbury in 1993 and Ellen DeGeneres in 2001.) Lynch has taken on the male world in other ways, too—most notably by playing roles originally meant for men. Her role in *The 40-Year-Old Virgin* (2005) was written for a man, as was the role she played in the 1993 blockbuster *The*

Lynch poses with a wax likeness of herself as Sue Sylvester at Madame Tussauds in Hollywood, California, in 2010.

Fugitive. In fact, her history of taking on male roles goes all the way back to high school, when she was cast as a king in a school play. Part of the reason she was sometimes cast in male roles in high school and college was that, at sixteen, she was already 6 feet tall—much taller than the other girls and even many of the boys. "I was difficult to cast," she admits. "I was still kind of a tomboy. I didn't look like a boy or a girl. I didn't carry myself as one thing or another."[5]

In addition to playing male roles, she also often plays very strong, dominating women, such as in *Role Models* (2008), as well as the part of Julia Child's sister in *Julie & Julia* (2009). Lynch believes that being "a completely unfeminine woman" has been key to allowing her to take on such roles. It has also been a factor in her success as an actor. But so has her willingness to go against the grain and challenge herself. "It's always a good idea to go up for the male roles," she says. "You go up against a bunch of beefy guys and the casting director then feels smart for taking you on, like he's the one who thought outside the box."[6]

After more than thirty years in a career that spans stage, film, and TV—as well as radio—she has become one of the most recognizable figures in entertainment today. Lynch is a talent that has definitely made her mark on American popular culture.

Chapter 1

A Desire to Be "Normal"

Jane Marie Lynch was born on July 14, 1960, in Dolton, Illinois, a middle-class suburb of Chicago. Her mother, Eileen, was a homemaker, and her father, Frank, was a banker. Jane was their second child. She has an older sister, Julie, and a younger brother, Bob. The Lynch home on Sunset Drive was always filled with plenty of humor and lots of singing.

A Midwestern Upbringing

Jane's father, who was of Irish ancestry, always kept the family entertained. Like the rest of the family, he loved to sing, and he would often come up with silly songs to make his children laugh. In addition to his frequent musical outbursts, Frank would dance around in the living room with his kids and make up goofy jokes to get the kids to laugh. "We would roll our eyes or feign embarrassment—but we all wanted to be the subject of Dad's silliness, to be a part of his joy,"[7] Jane says.

Jane's mother was half Swedish and half Irish, but her appearance was classically Swedish. She was tall, blonde, blue-eyed, and attractive—and Jane inherited these physical features. Although Frank could be very goofy, Eileen was very down-to-earth. She was a very frank, strong, and independent woman. "Our house ran like clockwork,"[8] Jane recalls. The family of five ate dinner together at the same time every night. They also attended Mass every Sunday at St. Jude's, a local Catholic church.

Julie was only two years older than Jane. The two girls shared a bedroom, which had green and yellow shag carpeting and a bedspread in the same colors. Despite their closeness in age, the two girls were very different from each other: Julie was a neat freak and Jane a slob. Julie loved to play with dolls and other typical little girl things. Jane, on the other hand, preferred to play catch outside with their father. Jane also enjoyed finding ways to torment her older sister—for example, one day she cut the belt loops off of Julie's favorite pair of jeans. Despite their frequent spats, Julie and Jane always wanted to sleep in the same bed together, which they did throughout their childhood.

Bob was two years younger than Jane. He was very quiet and tried hard not to do anything to bring attention to himself—unlike Jane, who loved to clown around just to get attention. Bob was also shy and was not very athletic, and Jane was only too happy to take his place outside, throwing a baseball back and forth with their father.

Jane's parents were very musical, singing all the time around the house. Her father would serenade her mother with Bing Crosby tunes in the kitchen, and the whole family would sing together on a daily basis, including Christmas carols and show tunes from productions such as *Funny Girl*, *Man of La Mancha*, and *The Sound of Music*. Jane particularly liked *The Sound of Music*; when this 1965 musical starring Julie Andrews came to their local theater, Jane went to see it one afternoon with her sister and two neighbor girls, and the four of them were so entranced that they wound up watching the movie over and over until Jane's mother picked them up that evening.

TV and Mediocrity

Even though the family followed a regular schedule, there was not much discipline or academic supervision. The three kids spent a lot of time watching TV, especially the popular sitcoms of the late 1960s and early 1970s such as *Gilligan's Island*, *The Brady Bunch*, and *Happy Days*. Jane also loved to watch comedian Carol Burnett, who had an early influence on her. Jane's

The 1965 hit movie The Sound of Music *was a favorite of young Jane, whose family enjoyed singing show tunes and other music together.*

love of ensemble comedy began to form while watching *The Carol Burnett Show* as a kid.

A big reason Jane watched so much TV is that she often did not feel understood or valued by those around her, including her teachers, friends, and family. She recalled years later that throughout her life she had "wanted nothing more than to be special and told 'You're exceptional.'"[9] In addition, she says, "I was always looking to be understood."[10] Part of how she dealt with the insecurity of feeling underappreciated was to escape into watching TV. She would daydream about going to California and becoming part of *The Brady Bunch* cast. She also pictured herself as a character on *The Mary Tyler Moore Show* and even wrote scenes in her head in which she and Mary hung out together. In Jane's fantasy world, she and Mary had "a very special relationship. . . . She had tenderness for me. I remember scenes where I'd go to Mary for advice and she'd tell me I was a very special child and nobody understood me, but she did."[11]

As a child, Lynch imagined she was friends with the Mary Richards character portrayed by Mary Tyler Moore (pictured) in The Mary Tyler Moore Show, *one of the television series Lynch loved to watch as a girl.*

Jane and her brother and sister loved to watch TV so much that they often neglected their homework, preferring instead to sit in front of the TV set after school. As a result, Jane's grades were mediocre all through school—mostly Bs and Cs. In fact, she barely passed her first semester of algebra in high school, and she flunked the second.

Her other achievements were mediocre, too. She was somewhat athletic—or at least tried to be—in junior high and high school. She was involved in many activities and clubs in high school, including basketball, girls' choir, tennis, theater guild, and the speech team. Yet although she was on the girls' basketball team—the Dirksen Junior High "B" team—she was a benchwarmer who rarely got to play. She also won several ribbons in junior high swim meets—most of them third place.

A Budding Actress

Jane first became interested in acting at age five when her parents took her to see a school play in which a neighbor's child was performing. Jane was fascinated by the experience: the stage, the lights, the actors in makeup. Everything seemed magical to her, like she was viewing another world. In particular, she was transfixed by a child in a cage who played a bird. "I remember thinking, *Let the bird out of the cage, let him out!* That's how real it was to me,"[12] she says.

In addition to this school play, Jane had other exposure to onstage performances. Her parents both loved to sing and perform, and they appeared in their church's annual show, *Port o' Call*. Jane was enthralled by the entire experience of putting on a performance, from the excitement backstage to the props and costumes onstage. She knew from an early age that acting was something she wanted to do. "For me, it was about being special and counting and also the world of make-believe,"[13] she recalls.

Then, when Jane was fourteen, she got the chance to speak to two of her idols when Ron Howard and Anson Williams, two cast members from the popular 1970s TV show *Happy Days*, came to Chicago to promote that show. Howard and Williams were making a guest appearance on a talk radio station, and

Jane called in and told them that she wanted to be an actress. Howard advised her to get some experience by appearing in plays and then, if she still wanted to pursue a career as an actress after college, to go to Los Angeles, California. Williams, however, offered more direct advice: He told her to get a list of agents from the Screen Actors Guild and start contacting them. Jane took this advice to heart, and on her next trip into Chicago with her parents, she convinced them to take her to the Screen Actors Guild office, where she obtained a list of talent agents in Chicago. Jane soon wrote letters to everyone on the list, as well as a letter to Universal Studios. She even wrote to the casting director of *The Brady Bunch* and included her school picture.

Contacting agents was pretty ambitious and unrealistic for a fourteen-year-old with no acting experience or training, but Jane did not realize it. After about six months, she finally got one reply, from an assistant casting director at Universal Studios. The letter was not very encouraging—it informed her that the studio only hired trained professionals with film experience. It also spelled her name wrong: Jamie. But Jane was thrilled just to get a letter from Universal, and she did not let her dreams be crushed by the rejection. She included the letter in her scrapbook.

Blowing It

Jane soon got the chance to follow Howard's advice and get some experience as an actress. In her freshman year in high school, she was cast as the king in the school play *The Ugly Duckling*. She was overjoyed and felt like she was on her way to fulfilling her dreams of becoming an actress.

But something happened when the rehearsals began. Jane suddenly became overwhelmed by an intense fear, and she began to worry that she would fail at the thing she wanted so much. "My first conscious memory was that I want to do that, [what] they are doing on television and [what] they are doing onstage," she says. "And when I got my opportunity I was so afraid of blowing it that I walked away from it."[14] She quit the play and—puzzled and confused by her own behavior—joined one of her school's sports teams so that she would have an ex-

Not like the Other Girls

When Jane Lynch was two years old, her brother, Bob, was born—and her father was thrilled. Finally, after having two daughters, he had a son who would play catch with him. As time went by, though, Jane's brother proved to be a shy boy who had no interest in athletics, while Jane wanted nothing more than to play baseball from morning till night. This sort of longing caused Jane to believe that her feelings and wants were not like other girls her age.

Jane's favorite time of year was Halloween because she could become anyone she wanted—and she always dressed as a male. She was a pirate, a hobo, and a ghost who wore a necktie. One year she dressed up as Orville Wright of the Wright Brothers, the famous duo who invented, built, and flew the world's first airplane. When Jane watched Disney movies, like many little girls she fantasized about being a part of them—but in her fantasies, she was the heroic prince, rather than the damsel in distress.

cuse to leave the play. "It was just . . . fear," she says. "It was as if I was walking up to my destiny, and I got scared and turned around and joined the tennis team."[15]

At the time, though, she did not understand what had led her to quit the play, and she felt like she had killed her dream. To make matters worse, because of her panicked decision, she was labeled as a quitter. Still longing deep down to be on the stage, however, she tried out for two more school plays that year but did not get a part in either one—not even a small part in the chorus. A classmate confided to Jane's sister that the reason Jane was not chosen was because she had quit *The Ugly Duckling*. Throughout the remainder of her high school years, she kept trying out for plays, but her reputation stuck with her. "I got little parts here and there but I wasn't able to shine because nobody trusted that I would stay in it," she explains. "I auditioned for everything and I got turned down. . . . It was terrible."[16]

Being labeled as a quitter was not the only challenge she faced in her early pursuit of becoming an actor. Jane's parents did not offer much encouragement, because they did not view acting as a suitable career. In their view it was something one did for fun, not as a means to earn a living. Her mother in particular told Jane that it was not realistic to think she could become an actress. She encouraged her daughter to learn to type so she would have something to fall back on. Because of this lack of support from her parents and because of her own insecurities, Jane stopped talking to other people about wanting to become an actress.

"I Really Felt Alone"

Jane always felt like an outsider, even in her own family. She longed to feel like she fit in somewhere but says that she grew up struggling with "a feeling of alienation—I was born thinking I came from another planet."[17] Feeling like no one understood her, she would often fling herself onto her bed in tears. She also sometimes dealt with these scary feelings by turning to humor. For example, she would joke with her family about having been adopted.

The feeling she had long had of being different, odd, and misunderstood was greatly intensified by a pivotal event in her life when she was twelve. Two girls in her class, twins named Jill and Michelle, came back from spring break in South Florida. The twins told Jane about something weird they had witnessed on the beach—two boys holding hands with each other. Then they told her with a measure of disgust that the boys were holding hands because they were gay. It was the first time Jane had heard the term or encountered the idea of homosexuality. "That's what I have," she thought. "I am the girl version of that."[18] In the next instant, she told herself that no one could ever know about it. The moment she learned what being "gay" meant and realized that she was gay, she also realized that other people would look at her differently if they knew. "I thought it was a sickness," she says. "I knew I had to keep it a secret."[19]

When she was growing up, Jane did not want to stand out. "I didn't want to be too tall. I didn't want to be too loud. I didn't want to be gay,"[20] she says. Her family so prized normality that Jane did not like the idea of being different. And, as she explains, "Nobody was gay. It wasn't talked about and I knew that I did not want to go out with boys. I knew I was different."[21] She adds, "I'm sure there were other gay people in my high school . . . but I really felt alone."[22]

Numbing the Pain

These feelings led Jane to keep two big secrets while she was growing up. One was that she wanted to be an actress; the other was that she was gay. The feelings of alienation, pain, and confusion she experienced as an adolescent were sometimes overwhelming. She found a way to cope with these feelings that was not healthy: She turned to alcohol.

Although she was underage, finding alcohol was not difficult. Jane grew up in a culture of drinking and cigarette smoking. Her parents loved to throw parties and served lots of alcohol. As a preteen, Jane would go downstairs after her parents' guests had left and sneak sips of their leftover drinks. She would also pick up discarded cigarette butts and relight them. Her father once caught her smoking outside the house when she was about twelve years old, but he did not scold her. Instead, Jane overheard him boast to her mother, "She's out there smokin' like a pro!"[23]

She started drinking more often when she was a freshman in high school—a beer or some Boone's Farm wine now and then. Drinking became a nightly ritual for her by the time she was a junior in high school. She and her friends would party every weekend and have keg parties at each other's homes. Although they had to hide their drinking at most of their homes, Jane and her friends drank openly in front of her own parents, who accepted and even encouraged it. Jane and her friends would sit around the family kitchen table with her parents, drinking and listening to her parents tell stories and sing old songs.

A Surprising Discovery

One day when Jane Lynch was eight years old, her little brother was listening to his transistor radio—a small, handheld radio with an earphone similar to those of a modern MP3 player, only for just one ear since it was not in stereo. Jane noticed that he kept switching the earpiece from one ear to the other, and she thought he was playing a joke on her. She was astonished to discover that her brother could hear with both ears, because she had only been able to hear out of her left ear for as long as she could remember. After a trip to the doctor, Jane and her parents discovered that a high fever she had had as a baby had led to nerve damage in her right ear.

Jane used her deafness as a way to get revenge on a school bully one day. Jane was a safety patrol officer; she wore an orange vest and helped make sure kids crossed the street safely on their way to school. One day the bully whacked her in the head as he walked past her. She grabbed her head and pretended he had damaged her good ear and left her completely deaf. Jane was thrilled when her prank landed the boy in trouble.

Gwiz and Trix

Jane had already begun drinking when she met Chris Patrick, the boy who would become her "boyfriend." They met at the beginning of their sophomore year in high school, at a dance at St. Jude's. She noticed him because he was smaller than the other boys and his hair was dyed bright red. The two were immediately drawn to one another. When Patrick—who also turned out to be gay—approached her across the dance floor, Lynch knew instantly they were soul mates. She recalls, "We quickly became inseparable best buds. We even gave each other nicknames—he was 'Gwiz' and I was 'Trix'—just because we thought nicknames were stupid, and it was fun to make fun of stupid things."[24]

Patrick and Lynch both had a terrific sense of humor. He loved to pull wild antics just to make her laugh—for example, making prank phone calls or tumbling down the stairs at school past her with his arms waving. But as close as they were, there was one thing they never discussed—the fact that they were both gay. Lynch was very, very closeted about her sexuality. Deep down she suspected that they were both gay but denied it to herself because she was not ready to accept it yet.

Lynch dated a few boys in high school and always tried to make it work. She felt like she should want the things the other girls she knew wanted: a boyfriend, marriage, and children. But no matter how hard she tried, she was never able to feel comfortable on a date with a boy and never felt physically attracted to a boy.

Although she often felt awkward around other people, with Patrick she was able to relax and be herself, and she felt like he would accept her as she was. In fact, there were very few times other than when she was with him that she felt at ease and good about herself. One of these was during choir class at school. She enjoyed singing and loved to hear the sound of many voices lifted together in song.

The other instance in which she felt at ease was when she was drinking—which also led her to experiment with marijuana. Lynch smoked pot for the first time in high school. Patrick did not tell her that he had laced it with angel dust (the street name for the illegal drug PCP). It made her start to hallucinate, and she wound up spending the night in his garage because she was too high to walk home. Lynch did not like pot, even without angel dust. She tended to avoid marijuana from then on, but continued to enjoy the escape of alcohol and drank regularly all through high school.

Godspell

Lynch and Patrick both loved the theater. Although she had been labeled as a quitter when she was a freshman, Lynch managed to get a few small roles in school plays the following year. She was often cast in roles intended for males, including as a police officer in *Arsenic and Old Lace* and a tomboy in *The Brick and the Rose*.

During her senior year, her theater arts class put on a production of *Godspell*. Lynch was very excited about appearing in the play. She and Patrick listened to the original cast album re-

Lynch appeared in a production of Godspell *during her senior year of high school. Being onstage gave her confidence and a feeling of belonging.*

peatedly and attended a live show at the Drury Lane Theater in Chicago at least ten times. Lynch loved the music, and she loved being part of the play and feeling like she was part of a team. Everyone pitched in, staying after school to help build the sets and to rehearse. "Being part of this group of fellow actors, feeling needed and valued and there for one another, was a high I would chase for the rest of my life,"[25] she says.

Part of what attracted her to acting was that in real life, she felt unworthy as a person, different, and awkward. Once onstage, however, she could slip into her role and become someone else, where all her own differences and inadequacies were hidden. She therefore felt that when she was onstage, she was safe from her fear of being rejected for who she was.

But then something happened with Patrick that would stay with Lynch for years to come. He became inseparable with a fellow cast member, Ed, and Lynch felt like she was being rejected. She responded by acting coldly and meanly toward Patrick. This was also the point at which she finally acknowledged to herself that Patrick was gay. She wrote him an angry letter in which she ended their friendship. She recalls:

> I was a stereotypical closet case, rejecting him for his open homosexuality that got him a boyfriend and left me alone. I pushed him away for what I was afraid of in me. Maybe I was also afraid of guilt by association, that other people would think I was gay, too. Whatever it was, I felt that he needed to be punished for flaunting his gayness. Didn't he understand you were supposed to keep it under wraps?[26]

Lynch felt heartbroken; Patrick had been her best and most trusted friend. When she lost him, she fell into despair. After Lynch graduated from Thornridge High School in 1978, she reluctantly set off to college, still smarting from the loss of her best friend. She was also still torn over her own identity and in deep denial about being gay.

Chapter 2

The Real Live
Jane Lynch

All through college, Jane Lynch struggled with her sexual identity and felt a great deal of self-recrimination every time she acted on her feelings toward other women. Although she experienced a great deal of inner turmoil during this time, she did pursue her dream of becoming an actress in college and graduate school. As a young adult, Lynch struggled to find her footing in her career, just as she also struggled to come to grips with her sexuality.

College in Normal

Lynch had grown up in a family that prized normality, and she wanted nothing more than to be normal. So it is fitting that she attended Illinois State University (ISU)—which is located in Normal, Illinois. Lynch was not particularly keen on the idea of furthering her education. "I wasn't interested in anything academically,"[27] she recalls. Her grades in high school were average, and she earned a low score on her college entrance exam. But her parents wanted her to go to college, and she had always been eager to please them. So, not knowing what else to do with her life, she set off for college at the only university that admitted her—ISU.

Her mother, who had never seen acting as a viable career choice, advised Lynch not to major in theater. Her mother told her instead to major in something similar to theater, such as mass communications. Lynch intended to do this, but when she went to register for her first mass communications class, it was full. Instead, she started taking acting classes and soon switched her major to theater arts—without telling her parents. In fact, her parents did not even realize she had switched majors until she auditioned for and won a talent-based tuition waiver; her parents got her tuition bill and saw that it was marked "paid."

During her second semester in college, Lynch tried out for a school play, a musical adaptation of the ancient Greek play *Lysistrata*. She was surprised and pleased that she was given a speaking role in the play, which was unusual for a freshman. She played Karmenia of Korinth, a hillbilly girl, and was very excited to be part of the production.

The following year Lynch got the chance to audition for *Gypsy*, another musical. After her audition, she figured that if she was cast at all, she would only make the chorus. She was stunned to discover that not only had she been cast but her name was on the principal cast list. She played Electra, a part that required her to sing a solo. She was extremely nervous about it. Yet unlike the time that she quit her first play in high

After high school, Lynch reluctantly attended Illinois State University, where she majored in theater arts.

FOUNDED 1857   ILLINOIS STATE UNIVERSITY

school out of fear, she worked really hard at rehearsals to learn her part and gained confidence in her voice. She also felt immense pride about being in the show, which felt to her almost like a professional production. These elements helped her stick with the play despite trepidation over singing a solo.

"I'm Gay Now, Too"

She had her first crush on a woman when she was a junior in college. But Lynch was still very much in denial about her sexuality, even to herself. When she would imagine kissing the woman, who was a professor at ISU, she always pictured herself as a boy. Nothing ever happened with her first crush, because the other woman was not gay. When the woman moved away at the end of the school year, Lynch fell into a depression that lasted her entire summer break.

When Lynch returned to school in the fall for her senior year, she developed a crush on another female professor. This time, however, the woman was also gay. Lynch was intrigued by the woman's unshaven legs, short-cropped hair, and most of all, her obvious comfort with being out of the closet. Although the woman was a professor, she was only ten years older than Lynch—and she liked to party with the students. Lynch's initial attraction to the woman turned into a mutual flirtation, which Lynch had mixed feelings about. One minute she was excited about what was happening; the next she was terrified by the implications: If she acted on her feelings for this woman, then there would be no more denying her own sexual orientation. Despite Lynch's ambivalence, the two of them soon developed a romantic relationship.

It was an emotionally tumultuous relationship for Lynch, who was still not comfortable with being gay. She alternated between being clingy and being aloof with the woman, between feeling elated and feeling ashamed about the relationship. When Lynch graduated from ISU in the spring of 1982, she took a summer job working in the cornfields outside of town so that she could be near her girlfriend. But when summer ended and she headed off to graduate school, the relationship came to an end.

After Lynch experienced her first romantic relationship, she managed to work up the courage to contact her old friend Chris

Patrick. The two of them had not spoken in four years, since she had ended their friendship in an angry letter. After pouring herself a stiff drink, she picked up the telephone and called him. She apologized for the letter and told him she missed him. "And I'm gay now, too,"[28] she confessed to him. Patrick forgave her and said he had always known she was also gay. The two of them rekindled their friendship and have remained friends ever since.

Culture Shock

Lynch had applied to and auditioned for several graduate programs in theater arts, and she was surprised when Cornell offered her one of only six graduate positions. Although Cornell, which is located in the town of Ithaca in upstate New York, was not the most prestigious actor-training program in the nation, it was an Ivy League school with a good reputation. She was thrilled to be able to study theater and acting for two more years, though she was nervous about living outside of Illinois for the first time.

Lynch attended graduate school at Cornell University in Ithaca, New York, to study theater. She struggled to fit in during her time there.

It was not long before the culture shock started to get to her at Cornell, and she felt miserable. Partly this was because she was not publicly out of the closet and experienced much angst and self-loathing about her secret. But it was also that she felt inadequate, like a country bumpkin. She made many blunders, such as trying to check out a rare, first-edition book from the library; the book was off-limits to students because of its exceptional value. She was out of her element in many ways at Cornell, too, and experiencing many things for the first time, such as different types of food she had never eaten, like tacos, bagels, and Greek food, and meeting people of diverse backgrounds.

She was on her own, far away from home, and she continued to suffer from low self-esteem and self-doubt. She also lacked confidence in her acting abilities. "My insecurities were heavy even then," she says. "I was dying to shine, but afraid to."[29] Lynch felt so bad that one day she tried to call in sick to class; the secretary told her that no one ever called in sick to Cornell's theater arts program, but Lynch stayed home anyway. In part to ease the distress she felt, she continued to drink heavily while at Cornell, downing an entire six-pack of Miller Lite every night.

Rocky Beginning

After graduate school, Lynch moved to New York City to try to make it as an actor. Her career, however, got off to a slow start. In fact, her first job out of school had nothing at all to do with the theater. She got a job in New York at Creamer Incorporated, an advertising agency owned by a friend's father. She worked in the public relations department—an industry she knew nothing about. Her job consisted mainly of sitting at her desk and doing things like cutting out press clippings and pasting them onto pieces of paper to show to her two bosses, who always praised her for doing a good job.

Unlike her two kind employers at the advertising agency, however, New York City felt very inhospitable to Lynch. She did not have an agent, so it was difficult for her to land auditions. She managed to get cast in a few off-off-Broadway shows, in which she took small parts that she felt were beneath her talent and for which she was usually unpaid. These shows often flopped and closed after only a couple of nights, at which point Lynch would go back to scrambling to get an audition somewhere else.

In addition to struggling to get established as a professional actor, Lynch also had a hard time finding a place to live. Her first apartment was a one-bedroom rental that she shared with a graduate student from Cornell. There was only one bed, so the two of them took turns sleeping on the couch. They sublet the apartment—meaning they were renting the apartment from a tenant with a lease, rather than from the landlord. When Lynch's sublet ended after a few months, she moved again and again, always leaving after only a few weeks or months. She went through five sublets in nine months. She had no car, so she would have to move all her belongings on the subway, which was difficult. Her roommates and their friends were not always nice people; several times she had cash or other items stolen. Once, she was kicked out of her apartment by the landlord, who told her she was subletting the apartment illegally and had to leave. Another time, two of her roommates in a large apartment in Brooklyn came home drunk one night and angrily ordered her out. Lynch, who never felt safe while she lived in New York, was terrified of being put out on the street in the middle of the night. She begged her roommates to let her stay, and they finally stumbled out the door and left her alone.

Lynch was unhappy the whole time she lived in New York. Just as she had since high school, she drank heavily during this time to help deal with the stresses she faced in her difficult situation. Eventually, the strain began to take a physical toll on her. One morning on her way to work, she found herself doubled over on the subway with sharp pains in her stomach. Afraid she had food poisoning or appendicitis, she headed for a nearby hospital. On the way, "hunched over in the worst pain of my life," she recalls, "I suddenly thought, *I have to leave New York. I have to get out of here.*"[30] With that realization, the pain in her stomach eased. Instead of going to the hospital, she went back to her apartment, packed her suitcases, and called her mother to tell her she was moving back in with her parents.

Becoming a Real Actress

Lynch was twenty-five years old when she moved back to Dolton to live in her old bedroom. Her mother immediately started suggesting that she try to find regular employment, perhaps as a secretary. Her mother was now a secretary herself, at an accounting firm called Arthur Andersen. But although Lynch held a graduate degree, she had never learned to type and did not know anything about writing a business letter. So when she went to interview at Arthur Andersen, she failed the secretarial tests she was given, much to her mother's embarrassment. She did manage to find a receptionist job, however—at the Civic Opera House in Chicago.

Chicago's Civic Opera House is where Lynch worked after college as a receptionist while she auditioned for acting jobs.

Lynch loved working in a theater, even if it was only as a receptionist. She also auditioned for several acting jobs and soon landed a part in an outdoor production of William Shakespeare's *The Comedy of Errors*. The play was staged in Lincoln Park near the shores of Lake Michigan. She played Adriana, a character who suspects her husband of being unfaithful. It was a big role, and her entire family came to opening night; it was the first time any of them had seen her act since high school. Lynch felt very lucky to be performing in a Shakespeare play, and the evening was one she will never forget.

The production turned out to be a pivotal moment in Lynch's life, and not just because she enjoyed the experience of being onstage so much. For the first time in her life, she stood up to her mother about her chosen career path. After the play ended, while her whole family congratulated her on her fine performance, her mother remarked that Jane should become a teacher. Lynch replied firmly, "Mom, you cannot ever say that to me again."[31]

Honing Her Improv Skills

Lynch stayed with the Shakespeare company for its production of *A Midsummer Night's Dream* the following year. But she was not getting paid for her performances, and she needed an income. So she auditioned for the TV home-shopping show *America's Shopping Place* and was hired. She and her cohost, Kendy Kloepfer, appeared live and talked about various products until well after midnight. They would talk back and forth about whatever products they were selling, such as clocks or cubic zirconia jewelry, and had to make up their dialogue as they went along. Although she did not realize it, her experience on *America's Shopping Place* turned out to be an excellent opportunity for her to hone her improvisational skills.

She soon got the chance to put these improv skills to better use. While working for *America's Shopping Place*, she landed an audition with an improvisational comedy theater called The Second City. She was cast as one of the members of the theater's

The Second City Comedy Troupe

The Second City was the first improvisational theater company in the United States. Its founders opened the doors of a small Chicago cabaret theater on a snowy December night in 1959. They quickly became known for an edgy brand of comedy that catered to the younger generation rather than conforming to the conservative norms of the time.

In the more than five decades since its debut, The Second City has launched the careers of Dan Aykroyd, Rachel Dratch, Tina Fey, Amy Poehler, Jack McBrayer, Mike Myers, and hundreds of other comedy actors. The comedy troupe, which has won numerous awards, entertains more than a million people each year in the United States and Canada, as well as other countries in Europe, Asia, and the Middle East. In addition to performances, The Second City's improvisational training centers offer classes to adults and teenagers who dream of becoming tomorrow's stars of comedy.

new touring company. Lynch was very excited to finally have a paying job as an actress. She says that The Second City was "perfectly suited to my skill set. I love sketch [comedy], I love improvisation, I love working in an ensemble."[32]

She stayed with the group for three years, touring with many other actors who also went on to have impressive careers, including Steve Carell, Stephen Colbert, Amy Sedaris, and Tim Meadows. In addition to being in the touring company, Lynch served as an understudy for the theater's main stage in Chicago. She was called upon to fulfill this duty several times, but Lynch ached to appear on the main stage in her own right. She frequently asked the producer about casting her, but after three years the producer finally told her she would never be a regular cast member at The Second City. After working so hard for so long, Lynch was devastated by the producer's words. "It broke my heart,"[33] she recalls. Lynch quit right then and there.

It was not long before she found a new home. Thanks to the experience doing improv with The Second City, she was cast in Chicago's prestigious Steppenwolf Theatre Company. Lynch was cast in a series of short plays; in the first of these, *Terry Won't Talk*, she played a role written for a man. She worked her way up as an understudy for a couple of plays and was cast as a regular in *Reckless*, a dark comedy. During her ten years with

Chicago's Second City comedy theater has been a proving ground for many popular comedians. Lynch spent time as a performer with the theater's touring company.

Steppenwolf, she also started doing voiceovers for TV and radio commercials, as well as appearing in TV commercials. "I was finally making a living doing what I loved, partly because I was willing to take just about any job."[34]

Living Out a Childhood Fantasy

In 1990 a friend from The Second City touring company invited Lynch to join a new show based on one of Lynch's favorite TV shows from her childhood, *The Brady Bunch*. Called *The Real Live Brady Bunch*, the show featured campy but faithful reenactments of various episodes of the TV show. Staged every Tuesday evening in a large, converted storefront called The Annoyance, the show quickly became a sensation, with people lined up around the block to plunk down seven dollars for a ticket.

Lynch played the part of the mother, Carol Brady, which had been played by Florence Henderson on the TV show. The cast scoured secondhand stores for 1970s clothing to use as costumes, which were all very informal; Lynch's blonde wig was held in place with a piece of yellow yarn. Like the other cast members, Lynch sometimes sang onstage. "I'm not a *great* singer, but I love to sing,"[35] she explains. The fact that she was singing songs from one of her favorite TV shows only made the experience more fun for her.

The show was sold out every night, and eventually gained national attention and was written up in magazines such as *Newsweek* and *Rolling Stone*. When Sherwood Schwartz, the creator of *The Brady Bunch*, learned what was going on, he claimed copyright infringement and sent a cease and desist order to the group at The Annoyance. Schwartz, however, decided to pay the show a visit himself before shutting the production down—and what he witnessed convinced him to change his mind. Audience members, who shouted out the words to the show, treated him like royalty. The enthusiasm of the audience and the cast combined made him realize that the show was a true homage to his TV creation. As a result, *The Real Live Brady Bunch* was allowed to continue, and Schwartz charged only one dollar per week as a token royalty.

After Schwartz's stamp of approval, many of the actors who had appeared on the TV show paid a visit to The Annoyance, including Florence Henderson and four of the

Lynch, top row center, played Carol Brady in The Real Live Brady Bunch, *a campy stage retelling of the hit 1970s television series. The production became a cult hit in the early 1990s.*

The Steppenwolf Theatre Company

In early January 1974, at a suburban Chicago church, a group of three young actors founded a theater group called the Steppenwolf Theatre Company. They rehearsed in the church basement and then performed their first live production, a play called *And Miss Reardon Drinks a Little*. At the time they had no way of knowing how much their theater would grow—or that what they had created would someday become one of the most revered theater groups in the world.

Now composed of forty-three actors, playwrights, and directors, the Steppenwolf Theatre Company is internationally known for its stunning depth of talent. The group has won numerous prestigious Antoinette Perry Awards for Excellence in Theatre, better known as Tony Awards. Their productions have also earned the esteemed Pulitzer Prize in Drama as well as the National Medal of Arts, which was awarded to them by President Bill Clinton. Yet despite all their recognition and fame, Steppenwolf's founders will never forget their humble roots from nearly four decades ago, when all they wanted was to do what they loved: perform. "I don't remember thinking more than a week ahead," says cofounder Jeff Perry. "I don't think any of us did. I think we only thought to the next opening of the show."

Quoted in Paulette Beete. "Filling Their Souls: A Sense of Home with the Steppenwolf Theatre Company." *NEA Arts*, 2012. www.nea.gov/about/nearts/storyNew .php?id=03_filling&issue=2012_v1.

Chicago's Steppenwolf Theatre Company is one of the world's most acclaimed acting groups.

actors who had played the Brady children. Says Lynch, "I remember being onstage at The Annoyance doing *The Real Live Brady Bunch*, looking at my fellow performers all decked out in their Brady wear and wigs, their faces earnest and committed, and thinking *Can it get much better than this?*"[36] *The Real Live Brady Bunch* went on to become a cult hit. It eventually went to New York City, where it ran for ten months, and then to Los Angeles for a seven-month run. When the gig in Los Angeles was up, Lynch went back to Chicago. Her plan was to do more theater—but an unexpected opportunity soon came her way that would change the course of her career.

Jobbing Jane

The success of the *The Real Live Brady Bunch* allowed Jane Lynch to become a more prolific actress. She worked hard during the 1980s, 1990s, and early years of the new century by taking almost every job that came her way. Lynch referred to herself during this time as a "workaday actor,"[37] meaning a character actor who takes on bit parts—any part—just to keep working. Thanks to her diligence, she gained experience and began to earn a reputation among directors as a fine character actress who was sought after for everything from commercials to sitcoms to bit parts in movies. Although she guest starred in numerous sitcoms over the years, she longed for something more permanent. Despite her many bit roles, however, she did not gain widespread fame in her career until she was in her late forties.

During this time, Lynch worked really hard. The experience of being branded a quitter after she dropped out of her first play in high school stayed with her, so she rarely turned down any acting job that came her way—whether it paid or not. She took virtually every job that was offered to her, no matter how silly the part or how slipshod the production. She explains: "I worked for free a lot. I did stuff I thought was stupid. Even for free I did things I thought were stupid. I'd do things to help a friend out. . . . And I'd be rolling my eyes, knowing how disorganized it was going to be and that I'd have to bring my own clothes."[38] But she always agreed. "I spent many, many, many years saying yes—to everything,"[39] she says.

A Big Break

Lynch was making good money as a character actress, appearing in plays and TV commercials and doing voiceovers for radio commercials. She even had a bit part in two movies in 1988. The first, *Taxi Killer*, folded before production was completed and was never released. Lynch also appeared in the comedy *Vice Versa*, which turned out to be a box office flop. Despite the disappointment of her first two films, she felt content with her success as a jobbing actor—one whose career bounces from one job to the next. But her career was about to get a big boost.

Her agent called to tell her she had been offered a small but significant part in a movie that was going to be filmed in Chicago—*The Fugitive*, starring Harrison Ford and Tommy Lee

A small role in the 1993 hit The Fugitive *starring Harrison Ford gave Lynch's confidence and career a significant boost.*

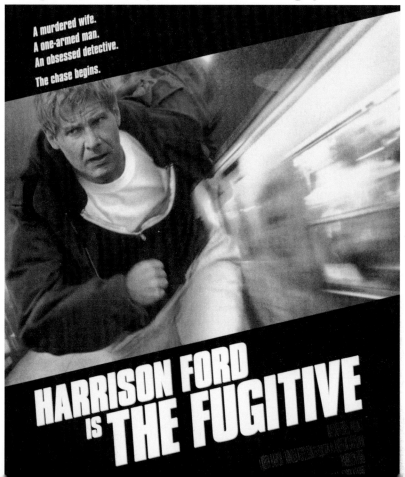

A murdered wife.
A one-armed man.
An obsessed detective.

The chase begins.

HARRISON FORD IS THE FUGITIVE

Impossible Not to Laugh

Chris Colfer is the young actor who plays Kurt Hummel in the popular television show *Glee*. In an April 2010 interview, Colfer talked freely about how this is the first job he has ever had (except for part-time work at a dry cleaner), described what it is like to be a part of a hit TV show, and shared some of his favorite behind-the-scenes moments.

One of the questions he was asked was whether he finds it hard to get through scenes with Jane Lynch without losing his focus and dissolving into fits of laughter. Colfer could not even answer the interviewer's question without laughing. "Yes, absolutely!" he said. "It's probably the hardest thing any of us have to do. She is so funny, and she will adlib and go off the script. Even things she says to you in between scenes are hysterical. She's a comedic genius and it's so hard. Sometimes you have to think about something really, really horrible like a tragedy of some kind just to get through it, because she's just that good."

Quoted in Allison Kugel. "Glee Star Chris Colfer Shares His Best Behind-the-Scenes Moments and Surreal Adventures." PR.com, April 26, 2010. www.pr.com/article/1151.

Jones. A friend of Lynch's who had seen her perform onstage had recommended her to the director, Andy Davis, who cast her in the role of a forensic scientist. For playing the part of Kathy Wahlund—a role originally written for a man—Lynch was paid eight thousand dollars, which seemed like a lot of money to her at that time.

Lynch was a bit starstruck by Ford because he was such a huge movie star. She was very nervous when they met on the set, which was compounded by the awkwardness of her not initially hearing him call out her name because he approached her on her deaf side. But Ford turned out to be a very considerate person, and Lynch felt comfortable working with him. The two of them retired to his trailer one rainy afternoon to discuss their most important scene together and iron out how they would play it. Lynch recalls, "I couldn't stop thinking, *I'm holding my own with Harrison Ford.*"[40] He even gave her several bits of acting advice throughout the filming that she has followed to this day.

Jobbing in Hollywood

The Fugitive turned out to be a blockbuster that was nominated for several Academy Awards, including Best Picture. After appearing in such a successful film, Lynch decided it was time to take her career to the next level. So, at age thirty-three, she moved from Chicago to Los Angeles. She took a studio apartment in Beachwood Canyon, a community in Hollywood, ground zero of the movie industry. Due in large part to the recognition she received when *The Fugitive* opened in the fall, Lynch began landing jobs right away. She did theater, guest starred on sitcoms, appeared in commercials, and did voiceover work. She appeared on countless series, including *Frasier*, *Friends*, and *The X-Files*. She also had a bit part as a reporter in the Carl Reiner film *Fatal Instinct* (1993). She says, "I felt successful all the time—even though nobody knew who I was."[41]

During this same time, Lynch created a character she called the Angry Lady and came up with a comedy routine that she performed at clubs. The Angry Lady would recount some injustice done to her and always had some sort of injury. "She was always wearing a neck brace, and she was always in the process of suing someone,"[42] Lynch says.

Lynch found that she enjoyed writing and performing her own material, and soon she started writing for other characters that she had made up. She spent about six months writing the script for a comedy act called *Oh, Sister, My Sister!* The show consisted of a series of female characters Lynch had created, including the Angry Lady, each telling their own tale of overcoming adversity. Lynch asked several of her friends to take on supporting roles and to help direct and produce the show.

Oh, Sister, My Sister! opened in 1998 at the Tamarind Theater in Hollywood. Its first performance was sold out. The show, which continued to be sold out through its entire eight-week run, received enthusiastic reviews and was named a pick of the week by *LA Weekly*. It also won the Best Comedy Ensemble of the Year Award from *LA Weekly*. The show's success brought Lynch some newfound confidence: "I had created and put on my own show,"[43] she says proudly.

A Breakout Role

By the time she wrote and performed *Oh, Sister*, Lynch was already a talented and well-respected character actress who was sought after by producers and casting directors. But she was still confined mostly to TV commercials, guest spots on sitcoms, and bit parts in movies. Soon after her show finished its run at the Tamarind, however, a lucky coincidence occurred that would change all that.

One morning, quite by chance, she ran into Christopher Guest, who had directed her in a Frosted Flakes commercial several months earlier. This chance encounter in a Los Angeles coffee shop led her to land what would be her breakout role. Guest was making a movie called *Best in Show* and invited her to be in it. The movie was a mockumentary, or mock documentary, a genre that Guest excelled in producing. There was no script and no rehearsals, only an outline written by Guest and Eugene Levy, who also appeared in the movie. Lynch's improv skills came in handy during the filming. She played a lesbian dog handler opposite Jennifer Coolidge, an actress Lynch had long admired.

Best in Show put Lynch on many audience members' radars for the first time. She went on to appear in two other Guest projects. She played a folksinger in *A Mighty Wind* (2003), in which she did her own singing and guitar playing, and in 2006 she played a tabloid journalist in *For Your Consideration*. With the success and popularity of these three films, Lynch's movie career began to take off—and she is quick to thank Guest for the part he played in her career. "The man changed my life," she says. "He blew the doors open for me."[44]

One of the Guys

Lynch's involvement in the Guest mockumentaries led to her appearance in several mainstream comedies over the next few

Lynch relied upon her improv skills to star as a lesbian dog handler opposite Jennifer Coolidge, right, in the mocumentary **Best in Show** *in 2000.*

years. The first of these was the 2005 hit *The 40-Year-Old Virgin,* which was cowritten and directed by Judd Apatow. She appeared in this comedy along with Paul Rudd, Seth Rogan, and her old friend from Second City days, Steve Carell, who had the title role. Lynch played the part of the manager of an electronics store where Carell's character worked. Her part was originally written for a man, but Carell's wife, actress Nancy Walls, said there were too many men in the movie and suggested that Lynch audition for the role.

As with the Guest films, much of the dialogue was improvised. For example, during her audition, Lynch decided it would be funny if the store manager tried to seduce Carell's character. "I came on to him and offered myself to him as his very first . . . sexual experience, let's call it,"[45] she says. The ad-libbed scene worked so well that it was written into the script. Also included in the film was a "Guatemalan love song," which Lynch wrote herself, using a dialogue from her high school Spanish class as the lyrics. She explains: "It has nothing to do with love; it's, 'Whenever I clean my room, I can't find anything. Where are you going with such haste? To a football game."[46]

The 40-Year-Old Virgin was a hit with audiences and reviewers alike. Movie critic Roger Ebert described it as "surprisingly insightful, as buddy comedies go," adding that "it has a good heart and a lovable hero."[47] With the success of this film, Lynch found her popularity began to rise. She appeared in a succession of buddy movies in which she was the sole funny woman in a group of guys. In 2006 she played another quirky female character in Talladega Nights: The Ballad of Ricky Bobby, another Judd Apatow production. She was the straitlaced Christian mother of NASCAR driver Ricky Bobby, played by Will Ferrell. As with The 40-Year-Old Virgin, much of the dialogue was improvised. The film was another huge hit, and reviewers applauded it. One reviewer described it as "more than just the year's funniest film, Talladega Nights is one of the films of the year."[48]

Lynch starred as the boss of Steve Carell's character in the 2005 film The 40-Year-Old Virgin, *a role that increased her popularity with movie fans.*

Lynch continued her string of buddy movies by playing a cocky drug rehabilitation counselor in *Role Models*, which starred Paul Rudd and Seann William Scott. This film really showcased Lynch's dry sense of humor. Her character is a recovering drug addict who claims she used to have cocaine for breakfast, lunch, and dinner. After the movie came out, audiences really identified Lynch with this role—so much so that she was frequently approached by fans and asked what she had for breakfast that day. She says, "It took me a while to realize they just wanted to hear me sneer 'cocaine.'"[49] Reviewers, too, found her performance memorable. One described it as "one of her most insane performances yet" and called her "one of the most recognizable comedic actresses of the decade."[50]

Critical Praise for *Julie & Julia*

Audiences and movie reviewers were not the only ones taking note of Lynch, thanks to her involvement in these buddy flicks. When director Nora Ephron saw Lynch in *The 40-Year-Old Virgin*, she called it "one of the most remarkable performances I've ever seen."[51] In 2009 Ephron began work on the film *Julie & Julia*. This movie portrays the life of Julia Child, an American woman who studied cooking in Paris and became a well-known chef. Ephron had already cast screen legend Meryl Streep as Child and immediately thought of Lynch for the part of Dorothy, Child's sister. Said Ephron, "The great Jane Lynch, whom I've wanted to work with for years and years and years. One of the great comic actresses. . . . I took one look at her and thought, 'Oh, she has to play [Julia's] sister."[52] Although this was a much more serious film than the buddy flicks Lynch had been featured in, there was a certain level of humor involved. Julia and Dorothy had a very close, loving relationship in real life, so even though the role Lynch was offered was small, it was an important part of depicting Child's life.

Julia and Dorothy were both over six feet tall in real life. Streep, who is only five feet six inches tall, had to wear huge platform shoes and specially designed clothing to make her appear taller in the movie. But even with the platform shoes, Lynch was still noticeably taller than Streep was. In fact, in order to get their heights to match better, Lynch went barefoot in their first scene together.

Lynch was nervous about working with Streep, Ephron, and the other actors in the film. "The caliber of the group had me reeling a bit," she says, "yet it also invigorated me. I relished the challenge ahead."[53] Lynch appeared in only a few scenes, but she earned high critical praise for her work in the film. Reviewer Michael Slezak described Lynch's performance as Child's sister as "beautifully gawky" and said Lynch did a masterly job of portraying "all the mysterious joy and excitement of sisterhood."[54] Slezak also called for Lynch to be nominated for an Academy Award for Best Supporting Actress, which did not happen, although Streep and the film itself were nominated for a number of awards.

Big Laughs on the Small Screen

At the same time Lynch was making a name for herself as an outstanding supporting actor in movies, she also continued to make many TV appearances, which brought her further attention. She made guest appearances in hit series such as *Arrested Development*, *Boston Legal*, *Dawson's Creek*, *Felicity*, *Friends*, *Gilmore Girls*, *Monk*, *The New Adventures of Old Christine*, and many others. Lynch's face—as well as her keen timing and wry sense of humor—were becoming a staple on the small screen as well as the large.

These were all guest spots and therefore temporary, however. "I would show up for one day or maybe five," she says. "I was grateful to have the work."[55] As always, Lynch took any role that was offered her. This sometimes led to some uncomfortable situations during filming. For example, in 2006 she guest starred on an episode of the TV murder mystery series *Night Stalker*. She played a lab technician, and in one scene, she had to hold a lab rat. "It kept biting me," she says, "and they insisted that we keep shooting."[56] Lynch did, indeed, continue with the scene, but she was a little worried when the producer called her the following

Lynch (left) played opposite Meryl Streep and Stanley Tucci in Julie & Julia in 2009. Although her role was small, her performance was acclaimed by critics.

week to ask whether she had gotten a tetanus shot. Fortunately, though, there were no serious consequences from being bitten by the rat.

After so many guest spots, Lynch hoped for something that would last through more than one or two episodes so she could settle in and develop her character a bit more. Beginning in 2004 she got that chance when she began to be cast in longer-term roles on TV. She played a recurring role as a therapist

Lynch portrayed Linda Freeman, a therapist who worked with Charlie Sheen's character on the hit television comedy **Two and a Half Men.**

in thirteen episodes of the hit TV sitcom *Two and a Half Men*. She played the sarcastic, sharp-tongued Linda Freeman, who frequently went one-on-one with Charlie Sheen's character in counseling sessions. Lynch called *Two and a Half Men* "one of the most wonderful sets to work on."[57] In 2010 she was recognized for her performance on the show with an Emmy nomination for Outstanding Guest Actress.

From 2005 to 2009 she had a recurring role spanning fifteen episodes of the Showtime drama *The L Word*, playing a feminist lesbian lawyer named Joyce Wischina. The show broke new ground, as a writer for the *New York Times* points out: "Before *The L Word*, lesbian characters barely existed in television."[58]

The Role of a Lifetime

By 2009 Lynch had been in more than sixty TV shows and sixty movies. Yet despite her success, she still longed for a more permanent home—and a steady paycheck. She got that opportunity when she was offered a part in the pilot for a new show on Fox called *Glee*. One of the show's creators, Ryan Murphy, had decided that his new, upbeat show about a high school glee club needed a villain. So he created the part of cutthroat cheerleading coach Sue Sylvester and proclaimed, "I think we can get Jane Lynch."[59]

Lynch became a household name in 2009 after she was cast as menacing cheerleading coach Sue Sylvester in Glee.

As soon as Lynch saw the script, she wanted to be part of the show. Unfortunately, she was already committed to do a pilot for another new show on ABC with Damon Wayans. She shot the pilot for *Glee*—in which she actually ad-libbed several of Sue Sylvester's lines—as a guest star, and she continued working on further episodes as a guest performer without knowing whether she would be able to continue. Lynch knew this was the role of a lifetime for her, and she desperately wanted to be a permanent part of *Glee*. During the shooting of the third episode, Lynch finally got a call from her agent telling her the producers of the other show had abandoned the project and released her from her contract. She was free to be a regular cast member on *Glee*.

Being a regular cast member has allowed Lynch to bring the character of Sue Sylvester to life. As the surly coach of the McKinley High School cheerleading squad, the Cheerios, Sylvester has made it her personal goal to squash the hopes and dreams of the kids who are in the school's glee club. She views the glee club sponsor, Will Schuester (played by Matthew Morrison), as her archenemy. Lynch says the producers "took their inner mean girl and created Sue Sylvester. And I get to say the most heinous things." Sylvester, in fact, is over-the-top mean to everyone around her. "She really wraps herself around how mean she can be," Lynch says. "She'll walk by a kid with books, and knock them down, just to knock them down."[60]

A classic Sue Sylvester moment occurs in a memorable scene from the first season, in an episode titled "Laryngitis." Sylvester is approached at the school by Kurt, a student who urgently needs to talk to her. After a moment, she interrupts him and says, "You know what, I checked out of our conversation about a minute back, so good luck with your troubles, and I'm gonna make it a habit not to stop and talk to students because this has been a colossal waste of my time."[61]

For Lynch, one of the best parts about being on the show was when her idol, Carol Burnett, guest starred in an episode during the second season. She played Sue's mother, a former Nazi hunter. Another highlight of the show for Lynch was filming the

"I Can't Say It"

Jane Lynch is well known for being an animal lover. She serves as a celebrity spokesperson for People for the Ethical Treatment of Animals (PETA), an animal rights group she admires and loves advocating for. She has spoken out against the famous Westminster Dog Show because it promotes the breeding of animals while millions are euthanized each year in shelters. Having adopted multiple dogs and cats over the years, Lynch says that her love for animals has made her a better person. So when a *Glee* script called for her to make a cruel remark about a cat, she refused to say it.

Lynch had been reviewing the script for one of the upcoming episodes. She noticed that her character, the evil cheerleading coach Sue Sylvester, was supposed to tell Will Schuester (played by Matthew Morrison) that she was going to torment him. Lynch drew the line at going into detail about what was going to happen, as she explains: "I had one line where I said something about how I was going to torture Will and I would skin a cat in front of him. And I said, I can't—I can't say it." To Lynch's relief, the script was rewritten with no reference to harming animals.

Quoted in Lauren Parvizi. "Jane Lynch Refuses Cat-Skinning 'Glee' Script." *Daily Dish* (blog), *San Francisco Chronicle*, September 17, 2010. http://blog.sf gate.com/dailydish/2010/09/17/jane -lynch-refuses-cat-skinning-glee-script.

Lynch, a passionate animal advocate, cuddles a dog at a pet adoption event in 2013.

video for "Vogue," in which Lynch as Sue Sylvester performs as Madonna. Lynch rehearsed tirelessly to learn the dance moves for the video, which turned out to be a huge hit with *Glee* fans.

An Overnight Success

Glee was an instant hit and quickly became a phenomenon, with the pilot episode going viral on the Internet. Fans called themselves "Gleeks" and took to social media to discuss their love of the show. An array of *Glee* merchandise appeared, including soundtracks, DVDs, clothing, young adult novels, and even the fictional autobiography of Sue Sylvester. Almost immediately after their debut, *Glee* and Sue Sylvester had become part of American pop culture.

Reviewers raved about the show—particularly about Lynch. As one reviewer put it, "One of the best things about the show can be summed up in two words: Jane Lynch. Her Sue Sylvester . . . is so deliciously self-absorbed, calculating and evil that she turns just about every scene into a delight."[62] For her role on *Glee*, Lynch has earned an Emmy Award and a Golden Globe and been nominated for countless others. Not everyone loves *Glee*, however. One columnist complained: "There's something repulsive about how they show kids suffering from one bigotry or another, then solve the whole mess with a couple of songs and a group hug."[63]

Criticism aside, at age forty-nine, Lynch seemed to have become an overnight success. This was no small feat—not many people that age are able to make such a huge splash in show business that they become virtually a household name. Noting that Lynch had finally hit it big after twenty-five years in the business, *Elle* magazine referred to her as the "hardest-working actress in TV."[64] For her part, Lynch agrees that she has worked herself very hard, but she believes that this is what she had to do in order to survive, not just as an actress, but as a person. She notes, "I was filled with angst all the time, but when it came down to it, I dove into what was in front of me and I always did my best. I invested 100 percent. And that's what saved me."[65]

Chapter 4

A Late Bloomer

After decades of trying, Jane Lynch's role as Sue Sylvester on *Glee* had finally allowed her to fulfill her childhood dream: to become a famous actress. But her path to this point was long and sometimes tortured. Lynch struggled throughout her twenties, thirties, and forties to gain control of her life and become fully adult. She finally managed to come to grips with her fear of failure and addiction to alcohol, but only after many setbacks and struggles.

Trying to Quit Drinking

When Lynch was in her mid-twenties, she had read a book called *The Seat of the Soul* by Gary Zukav. This book had a powerful effect on her. It helped her realize that she had always felt like she was at the mercy of fate—when in reality, she had the power to control her own life through the choices she made. Lynch immediately bought a copy of the book to send to her old friend Chris Patrick, who was similarly moved by the book's transformative message.

The first of her life's choices that she examined was one that she had avoided facing for several years—her excessive drinking. She knew that she was addicted to the Miller Lites she guzzled every night. She had been drinking regularly since her senior year in high school, and even though she continued to function normally by showing up for work and paying her bills on time, she knew she had to do something about her alcohol consumption. "I had debilitating hangovers," she says. "It was a big problem."[66]

Lynch lifts her water glass for a toast at the Golden Globe Awards in 2011. After many years of addiction, she no longer drinks alcohol.

She decided to cut back on her drinking; instead of every night, she would only drink two nights a week. But this plan backfired, because on the nights she did drink, she wound up drinking even more than usual, as if trying to make up for the nights she had gone without.

Replacing One Addiction with Another

Then one night in 1991 she was sipping a glass of wine while talking on the phone with Patrick, who had been sober for several years. She had the sudden realization that she had to quit drinking altogether. "Something just clicked and I said, that's it," she recalls. So she walked over to the kitchen sink and poured her glass of wine down the drain. It was the last alcoholic drink she ever had. "It wasn't dramatic," she says. "I was struck sober. . . . I kind of got a plunk on the head and have been sober ever since."[67]

But living her life in sobriety proved to be a challenge. She had for years relied on Nyquil, a liquid cold remedy that actually contains alcohol, to help prevent or relieve hangovers. So when she quit drinking, she began dosing herself with Nyquil every night instead, because the medicine gave her a soft buzz and helped put her to sleep. Soon she was also taking Nyquil during the day and sleeping the afternoons away. "The fact that Nyquil had alcohol in it was not something I acknowledged,"[68] she says.

Then one night in 1992 at a cast party for *The Real Live Brady Bunch* in New York, some of the other cast members began to smoke marijuana. Lynch had tried marijuana a few times and never really liked it. But she smoked it that night, partly because she wanted to feel like part of the group and partly because she wanted to escape the inner confusion and loneliness she had always felt. And since she had given up drinking, she thought that smoking marijuana would give her the escape she sought. But the pot only made her feel worse, and she got up and walked home by herself. As she crawled into bed, she felt terrible.

A Life-Altering Decision

In the morning Lynch made a life-altering decision. She realized that she was still abusing substances—she had just substituted Nyquil and now marijuana for beer. So she got up and called Alcoholics Anonymous (AA), and she started attending the meetings faithfully every night. Attending meetings helped her realize that her decades-old drinking problem stemmed from deep-seated feelings of inadequacy and fears that she was not good enough. Ever since she was a child, she had believed there was something fundamentally wrong with her. She apologized constantly, even when she had done nothing wrong, and she thanked people effusively. She realized she acted this way because she felt as though she had to compensate for whatever it was in her that was broken.

One night while at an AA meeting, she was suddenly struck by the realization that everything could not possibly be her fault. Lynch felt a tremendous relief. "I realized that if I'm obsessing about my own feelings, I'm not present with the people around me—and am frankly of no use to them." AA helped Lynch assess a given situation and determine whether she was truly responsible for whatever was going on and often to realize that whatever she thought was her fault actually had nothing at all to do with her. This has "helped me become a better friend, a better partner, and a more helpful person,"[69] she says.

After eight years of faithfully attending meetings every night, Lynch no longer felt the urge to drink or to abuse Nyquil. She felt solid and stable enough to stop attending meetings but will always feel indebted to the organization for helping her get control over this part of her life.

A Confession

Lynch had known for a long time that her conflicted feelings over her sexuality contributed to her alcohol abuse. Drinking had been her way to numb the pain and confusion she had always felt about being "different." But being a closeted lesbian had another negative effect on her life: It affected her relationship with her family.

By the time she was in her early thirties, Lynch had become somewhat alienated from her family. Her relationship with her parents had become distant, and she barely corresponded with her brother and sister. She realized these relationships had deteriorated because she was keeping a huge secret about herself from them. Although she had confessed to her parents that she was an alcoholic and was attending AA meetings, she still had not told them she was gay.

Alcoholics Anonymous

In 1935 a meeting took place in Akron, Ohio, between a stockbroker named Bill Wilson and a physician named Robert Smith. Wilson had been sober for five months and was struggling hard to stay that way. Smith wanted to quit drinking but had not been able to—until he met Wilson, who inspired him to put down the bottle for good. The two men formed a bond and vowed to help others who struggled with drinking problems. In 1939 they published a book called *Alcoholics Anonymous*, and the organization they built took on the same name. The book described the group's philosophy and principles and explained the now-famous spiritually focused Twelve Steps. These include admitting one has an addiction, making amends for mistakes one has made in the past, and helping others who share the same addiction.

Over the years Alcoholics Anonymous, or AA, has grown into a worldwide fellowship with more than 2 million members in 150 countries. Members attend as many meetings as they want (on the basis of availability) and are encouraged to share their experiences, talk about their progress in working through the steps, and support others who are struggling.

New members oftentimes seek out a sponsor in the AA program who can offer one-on-one support to them in their efforts to recover from alcoholism.

A person wears an Alcoholics Anonymous "Ninety Days" tag to signify being sober for that long. Lynch turned to the organization for support to end her decades-old drinking problem.

Lynch recalls that she was "suffering so much over this alienation [from her] family"[70] that in 1992 she began seeing a therapist. The therapist helped her work through her feelings about her family and also helped her accept and embrace her sexuality. Most important, though, she convinced Lynch to write a letter to her parents in which she explained everything. The therapist stressed that Lynch would feel better just by writing the letter, even if she never sent it. So Lynch wrote an open and honest letter to her mother and father. "I wrote that I could feel us drifting apart, and that a lot of it had to do with who I was: that I was gay, and that although I hadn't had any real relationships yet, whenever I did it would be with a woman,"[71] she explains.

Lynch did feel better after writing the letter—so much better, in fact, that she decided to go ahead and send it. After her family read the letter, they were all very supportive of her. Her parents had both wondered whether their middle child was gay, but they had never discussed it with her or each other. By the time Lynch told them, at age thirty-two, that she was gay, they treated it as no big deal. "My parents were just wonderful about it,"[72] she says. "Had I told them when I was 18 it would have been a different story, because there was nobody openly homosexual [at that time]."[73]

Lynch had come out to her friend Patrick about a decade earlier, and now she had come out to her parents as well. But unlike many other homosexual actors, she was never deeply in the closet professionally, and so she never really had to deal with coming out as an actor. Coming out of the closet professionally for her was not a big deal for a number of reasons—in large part because she mostly did bit parts. "By the time I started to do work where people knew who I was, I just never made the choice to hide that I was gay,"[74] she explains. She also credits actress and comedian Ellen DeGeneres, who became a trailblazer by coming out in the mid-1990s, for paving the way for other actors to be open about being gay. Lynch also points out that because she is a character actress, it was easier for her to be open about her homosexuality. "If Julia Roberts were gay, I think it would be harder," she explains. "Because she's an ingénue. You want to project your hopes and dreams for love [onto her]."[75]

Comedian Ellen DeGeneres (pictured) is cited by many gay and lesbian actors, including Lynch, for blazing the trail for others in the entertainment industry to be open about their homosexuality.

Becoming an Adult

Although Lynch had taken charge of her life by quitting drinking and coming out to her parents, she still did not feel fully adult. In part, this was because she was still immature, she says. "I spent so much of my younger life drinking, and being drunk makes learning to be a grown-up kind of hard."[76] In addition, she still had very few adult responsibilities; for example, she had always rented rather than owned her own home, and she did her laundry at the corner laundromat.

By the time she was in her late thirties, she decided it was time to act like a real adult. One of the first things she did was adopt a cat, which she named Greta, after one of her childhood idols, movie star Greta Garbo. She soon adopted another cat, Riley, and then a puppy she named Olivia, after another idol of hers, actress and singer Olivia Newton-John. A few years later, she adopted another puppy, Georgie Girl. Now that Lynch had created a "family" for herself, she began to feel more responsible—as well as happier, because her companion animals brought so much love into her life.

Lynch and her dog Olivia attend a benefit event in 2006. She adopted Olivia and several other pets to create a family for herself.

She soon decided that it was time she bought a home for herself and her furry family. She found a house in Laurel Canyon, an area in the Hollywood Hills of Los Angeles, and immediately fell in love with its cobblestone path and inviting fireplace. So Lynch bought the house and moved her family of pets in. She says, "Cozily ensconced in my house with my animals and my very own washing machine, just a few months shy of my fortieth birthday, I finally felt like a grown-up."[77]

She set about decorating the house by buying furniture and painting the walls. She also overcame her lifelong aversion to tidying up after herself and began to keep her house and her things more organized. And she bought a TV for the first time in her adult life and started watching the news and becoming more aware of current events.

"Crazy About Each Other"

Lynch was a late bloomer in her personal relationships, too. For years her fear of being rejected, as she felt she had been with Patrick back in high school, led her to shun intimacy, and she would push people away if they got too close. One example of this was when *The Real Live Brady Bunch* was playing in New York and the other cast members got places together to save money on living expenses. But Lynch felt like too much of an outsider to ask to move in with anyone. "I could have piped up and asked, but I felt unable to deal with the possible rejection and humiliation of asking and being turned down,"[78] she confesses.

A big part of her fear of being rejected was her low self-esteem. She believed that once people got to know her, they would not like her. It was the same pattern with coworkers, friends, and lovers—in order to avoid the possibility of feeling abandoned, she would reject the other person first. It took her a long time to start building lasting friendships with people or to feel like she actually "belonged" with the rest of the cast on a project. In fact, it was not until she was touring with the cast of *A Mighty Wind* in 2003 that she stopped feeling like an outsider and instead felt that she deserved to be there.

Still, by the time Lynch was in her late forties, she had never had a serious, long-term romantic relationship with anyone. She had never lived with someone she was dating and had never thought of marriage or having children. All of that changed in 2009 when Lynch flew to San Francisco to present an award to a friend of hers at a gala for the National Center for Lesbian Rights. While there, she met psychologist Lara Embry, who was there to receive a Justice Award for winning a legal battle with her former partner over custody of one of their daughters. When Embry, who recognized Lynch from her role on *Two and a Half Men*, approached her for an autograph, the sparks flew between the two women. By the time the weekend came to a close, they had fallen in love and were making plans to see one another again.

Embry lived in Florida, and Lynch lived in California. During her first hiatus from *Glee*, Lynch flew frequently to Florida and spent lots of time getting to know Embry. She also got to know Embry's biological daughter, seven-year-old Haden. Lynch fell in love with Haden, too, and the three of them soon began to feel like a family. Before long, Embry suggested they get married.

Although deeply in love, Lynch had a few reservations about marriage. She was afraid of moving too fast—she and Embry had known each other for less than a year. She also worried about the effect getting married would have on Haden, especially if things did not work out. Plus, getting married was not as easy as it would have been for a straight couple—just a handful of states had legalized same-sex marriage by 2010, and neither California nor Florida was one of them. But Embry helped put her mind at ease about these issues, and Lynch finally agreed that the two of them should marry.

Still, she had one last concern. Lynch's father had passed away in 2003; "I miss him every day,"[79] she says. But she worried about how her eighty-year-old mother, Eileen Lynch, would take the news that her daughter was planning to marry another woman. Indeed, at first Eileen seemed not even to be aware that gay marriage was legal in certain places. Once she got over her initial surprise that such a thing was possible, however, Eileen was very supportive of her daughter's plans to get married.

Lynch and Lara Embry attend the Screen Actors Guild Awards in 2012.

Lynch and Embry were married on May 31, 2010, in Sunderland, Massachusetts—a state in which gay marriage is legal. The small, simple wedding was held on the patio of an old courthouse building that had been turned into the Blue Heron Restaurant. When it was Lynch's turn to recite her vows, she promised "to be the very best parent I can be" to Haden and

The Work

When Jane Lynch thinks about what helped her reach the major turning points in her life, she credits her discovery of a woman named Byron Kathleen Reid, more commonly known as Byron Katie. In 1986, after a long battle with severe depression and alcoholism, Katie was overcome by a profound realization: that her misery was the result of her own thoughts, not some force outside of her control. She suddenly became aware that the suffering in her mind was not reality and that she was torturing herself needlessly.

Katie, who is now a spiritual mentor to Lynch and millions of other people, went on to develop a unique method of self-inquiry called The Work. At the heart of the program is the idea that when people listen to and believe their stressful thoughts, they suffer. But by questioning those thoughts, they often find out that there is no basis for their negative feelings, which brings them a sense of joy and freedom from stress. "That's when we're home," says Katie. "The wait is over. The wanting and needing are all over when you find it's all inside of you."

Quoted in *Los Angeles Magazine*. "Ready to Get to Work? Bring It On!" October 2011, p. 176.

Byron Katie gained many followers with her self-help program called The Work.

also "to do my best to get her 'iCarly' [TV show] tickets."[80] After the ceremony, the newlyweds and their fifteen guests enjoyed an intimate dinner and wedding cake in the restaurant, where they were entertained by a four-piece jazz combo. They were also treated to a performance by Lynch and Haden to the dance moves from the *Glee* "Vogue" video, which Haden had tirelessly helped Lynch rehearse.

Lynch was thrilled to be in a committed relationship for the first time in her life. And she and Embry were deeply, madly in love with each other. "They're adorable together," said Cheyenne Jackson, who plays Dustin Goolsby on *Glee*, at the time, "doting, respectful, and just clearly crazy about each other."[81]

As much as Lynch had accomplished in her career up to this point, she sees her greatest achievement as her relationship with her wife. As Ryan Murphy, executive producer of *Glee,* comments, "[Lynch's] private life is probably more important to her than her work life, which is rare."[82]

Inner Peace

In a few years' time, Lynch became a recovering alcoholic who appeared to have gained happiness and tremendous personal growth beyond her expectations. For instance, as she approached age fifty, she had become resigned to the fact that she would never become a parent, but after marrying Embry, Lynch was overjoyed to discover that parenthood was still attainable. "[I] thought that possibility was behind me, so this is a real delight,"[83] she said of her opportunity to parent Embry's daughter, Haden.

It did not take long for Lynch to settle into her new roles as a wife and mother after Embry and her daughter moved into the Laurel Canyon home Lynch had redecorated to accommodate her new family. At the time Lynch said she had never felt more at peace. "It's not like I'm done growing, evolving," but, she adds, "[I have] more compassion and kindness for myself. And, you know, I have to cut myself some slack."[84]

Chapter 5

Activist Jane

Besides having more compassion for herself, Jane Lynch has a compassion for many charitable causes. She is actively involved in supporting and protecting several that are close to her heart. She has done public service announcements and other forms of activism for issues ranging from equal rights for gays, the welfare of animals, and the safety and education of young people. She also opened up her heart and, with the help of her wife, penned a frank and funny autobiography that gives a candid glimpse into her own life and character, including her many triumphs and failures.

"Things Do Definitely Get Better"

After years of inner struggles, today Lynch is very comfortable with her own sexuality, and she is particularly outspoken about gay rights. "When you get out there and you hear about people suffering at the hands of homophobia, it's shocking,"[85] she says. Lynch is deeply disturbed by homophobia (the fear or mistreatment of gay people) and the numerous ways in which gay people, especially gay youth, struggle or are targeted by those who hate or fear them. Gay youth are particularly prone to isolation, depression, bullying, and taking their own lives as a result of these pressures. It was these concerns that led her and Lara Embry to appear in a public service announcement (PSA) for the It Gets Better Project in 2010. This series of Internet videos was begun by journalist Dan Savage and his partner, Terry Miller, in order to give young people a message of hope.

In their video, Lynch and Embry sit side by side and talk candidly about their experiences growing up gay. They offer their encouragement to other young people who share their struggles. Says Lynch: "I realized I was gay when I was about twelve. I thought it was a disease and I had it. . . . It made me feel alone, because I felt like I had this deep, dark secret that nobody shared, and it had to stay a deep, dark secret. And I wish that I

Lynch, appearing at the Emmys with her Glee costar Chris Colfer in 2011, is proud of how the show portrays its gay characters in a positive light.

had known that if I hang in there things would get better. And today I can say that—things do definitely get better."[86]

In addition to her It Gets Better video, Lynch's involvement with *Glee* has offered gay or identity-confused teens a rare and much-needed role model. Although Lynch's character Sue Sylvester is not gay, *Glee* is a rarity for featuring an openly gay actress in a major role. In addition, Lynch's costar Chris Colfer and one of the show's creators, Ryan Murphy, are both openly gay. And Colfer's character, Kurt Hummel, is gay. Many gay fans identify strongly with the show because of the involvement of Lynch, Murphy, and Colfer and because the show positively portrays openly gay students. In one episode, for example, Colfer's character receives an apology from the boy who had bullied him, a closeted gay football player. The episode ends with the cast singing Lady Gaga's self-pride anthem "Born This Way." Although the episode was criticized by conservatives for promoting homosexuality, it was a huge hit with liberals and *Glee* fans. Lynch says most fans of Sue Sylvester who approach her are fourteen to fifteen years old, and many of them struggle with issues concerning their own sexuality. "It's really rewarding and satisfying," she said, "because this show has impacted kids, as I know you all know, like you wouldn't believe. [For] some kids, it's like they've been given a reason to live."[87]

Gay Rights Advocate

Lynch shows her support for gay rights in many ways. For example, she has been involved in Outfest, which is held every year in Los Angeles. It features a film festival showcasing gay-themed films and gives its Outie Award in sixteen categories, including screenwriting and acting. Outfest also presents the Outfest Achievement Award and the Outfest Honors, among many other accolades. In 2010 Lynch participated in an Outfest panel discussion to talk about her life and work as a lesbian. She spoke for ninety minutes about topics such as her decision to become an actress and the fame she has found on *Glee*.

In 2012 Lynch participated in the play 8 by the Academy Award–winning screenwriter Dustin Lance Black. The play portrays the federal trial that overturned Proposition 8, California's

The It Gets Better Project

In July 2010 journalist Dan Savage read about the suicide of Justin Aaberg, a fifteen-year-old boy from Anoka, Minnesota. Justin hanged himself after being relentlessly bullied by classmates because he was gay. Less than two months later a similar tragedy struck in Greenburg, Indiana. Fifteen-year-old Billy Lucas, who had also been bullied because of his sexual orientation, killed himself in his family's barn. Savage, who is gay, was sickened over the tragic and senseless deaths and knew he had to do something. "I was just stewing and writing about them on my blog, and wishing I could have talked to these kids, to tell them it gets better," he says.

So Savage and his partner, Terry Miller, created a video about their own experiences being bullied as teens and uploaded it to YouTube. Their goal was to get across a simple message to lesbian, gay, bisexual, and transgender young people: You are not alone, and it really does get better. Savage's idea grew into an enormously successful movement called the It Gets Better Project. Hundreds of gay and straight celebrities have contributed videos, including Jane Lynch, Anne Hathaway, Ellen DeGeneres, and Ke$ha, as well as political officials such as U.S. president Barack Obama, Vice President Joe Biden, and former secretary of state Hillary Clinton. By January 2013 more than fifty thousand user-created videos had been uploaded to the YouTube It Gets Better channel.

Quoted in Jessica Bennett. "Dan Savage and Jane Lynch." *Daily Beast,* December 20, 2010. www .thedailybeast.com/newsweek/2010/12/20 /dan-savage-and-jane-lynch.html.

Dan Savage created the It Gets Better Project to help lesbian, gay, bisexual, and transgender young people.

ban on same-sex marriage (in June 2013 the U.S. Supreme Court dismissed an appeal against Proposition 8 and gay marriages have resumed in the state). Lynch appeared onstage along with her *Glee* costar Matthew Morrison and several big-name performers, including actors George Clooney, Brad Pitt, and Jamie Lee Curtis. The play was performed at the historic Wilshire Ebell Theater and broadcast live on YouTube to help raise money for the American Foundation for Equal Rights. Lynch was very moved by the contributions of everyone involved in the play and said she was touched by "all these really big stars with fire power up there and advocating for our rights."[88]

Lynch has shown her support of gay rights and causes in other ways, as well. When New York legalized gay marriage in the summer of 2011, Lynch tweeted: "Yippee New York for gay marriage!"[89] And in 2012 she was vehemently outspoken against the restaurant chain Chick Fil-A for its stance against same-sex marriage. After the chain's chief operating officer made sev-

Lynch speaks at Outfest's opening night gala in 2008. She is an outspoken advocate for gay rights.

eral public statements condemning gay marriage, Lynch joined many celebrities, including *The Office* star Ed Helms as well as countless private citizens, in boycotting the restaurant. Facing a public relations disaster, Chick Fil-A eventually backed away from its stance. But it was not the last time Lynch and others would feel the need to stand up against discrimination against gays. Later in 2012 the president of the Amway company and his wife made a sizable donation to an antigay group, the National Organization for Marriage. Gay rights activist Fred Karger began a movement to boycott Amway, and when he approached Lynch for her support, he says that she "grabbed the pen out of my hand and signed away."[90]

Lynch has received accolades for her outspoken support of gay rights. For example, in 2005 she was named one of the 10 Amazing Women in Showbiz by the Professional Organization of Women in Entertainment Reaching Up, also known as POWER UP. And in 2012 she was named *Out* magazine's Entertainer of the Year.

Doing Her Civic Duty

In addition to being an advocate for gay rights, Lynch also champions other important causes. Lynch, who has several companion animals she loves dearly, has spoken up on behalf of animals on numerous occasions. For example, in 2010 she recorded a PSA for PETA (People for the Ethical Treatment of Animals) to encourage people to adopt animals from a shelter, rather than purchase them from a store. She recorded another PSA for PETA (along with one of her own dogs, Georgia) in which she encourages people to spay or neuter their animals. Lynch also wrote a letter in 2010 to Richard Daley, the mayor of Chicago, on behalf of PETA to ask for his support of a law to require dogs and cats in that city to be spayed or neutered.

Lynch is also involved in an effort to convince the Atlanta Pride Festival, a yearly gay rights event in Georgia, to switch the venue for its annual kickoff party to what she thinks would be a more animal-friendly location. The party has been held for several years at the Georgia Aquarium, which is home to many species of marine mammals. After Dan Mathews, vice president of PETA, attended the 2011 party, he warned that the loud music that booms from the many amplifiers disturbs the marine mammals, many of whom rely on sound to communicate, and asked the festival organizers to move it somewhere else. When the festival again scheduled its 2012 kickoff party at the aquarium, several people joined him in his campaign to move the party to a more humane location. Lynch wrote a letter to Buck Cooke, managing director of Atlanta Pride, on PETA's behalf, reminding him that marine mammals are "extremely sensitive to sound." She stated that large parties subject the animals to "an even more stressful environment than they already endure in captivity"[91] and that the noise levels disorient the animals and sometimes cause them to become aggressive toward each other. Despite the efforts of Lynch and PETA, however, the 2013 kickoff event was again held at the Georgia Aquarium in October.

Just as she loves animals, Lynch also loves children. As a parent, she is naturally concerned about the safety and well-being of kids, and she has undertaken several projects with kids in mind. She is featured in the LG Corporation's campaign called Text Ed with Jane Lynch to educate kids about the use of cell phones, such as the dangers of texting while driving, as well as sexting and bullying via cell phone. In the videos she plays a former "text offender" and delivers her lines with her usual dry humor. "Mobile bullying, text rage—you name it, I typed it up and hit Send,"[92] she quips. She added an extra warning via her Twitter account: "Don't text and drive, kids!"[93]

Another PSA Lynch has done with kids in mind is for the Adopt the Arts Foundation, which works to support funding for the arts in schools. The video, called "Epic School Battle," features kids from Rosewood Elementary School in Los Angeles, with Jane Lynch playing their teacher. The video features cameos by several well-known entertainers, including legendary rocker Steven Tyler.

Lynch has also taken on the task of educating young people and their parents about avoiding excessive student loan debt. She has helped launch the National College Finance Center, a nonprofit website that contains information on grants, schol-

Lynch appears at a PETA benefit in 2012. She has been a vocal supporter of the organization and other animal-rights causes.

arships, and loans, as well as information on how to pay off student loan debt. "It's a terrific resource for researching and finding the best student loan for you, so you can avoid majoring in debt,"[94] says Lynch. She wanted to get involved with this project because several of her nieces and nephews had taken on more student loan debt than they could afford to pay back.

Happy Accidents

In 2011 Lynch was involved in another project very close to her heart: writing her autobiography. She was inspired to write it after she and Embry appeared in their PSA for the It Gets Better Project. Lynch said she wrote the book by "spending a lot of time inside my head in a closed room."[95] In the book, Lynch details her life growing up in Dolton and gives a warm and funny portrayal of her family members. She also delves into the pain and isolation she experienced for years over her sexual orientation, as well as her battle to overcome her alcohol addiction. The book also details Lynch's path to becoming a professional actor, stressing that she has gotten where she is today because of a series of fortunate coincidences that she terms "happy accidents," a phrase she chose to be the title of the book.

Lynch cowrote the book with Embry, who thoroughly enjoyed sharing the creative process with her. "We've been cracking up over it writing it together,"[96] said Embry. *Happy Accidents* became a best seller. A writer for *Vogue* magazine called it a "frank, engaging, and at times uproariously funny autobiography of a roller-coaster life."[97] For her part, Lynch says, "Any time you write truthfully about yourself, I think people latch on to it. They don't have to have exactly the same experience to have it resonate for them."[98]

In addition to the assistance of her wife, Lynch was very excited by the contribution her idol and pal Carol Burnett made to her autobiography. "Can I just say how honored & just plain thrilled I am that CAROL BURNETT wrote the [foreword] to my book,"[99] Lynch wrote on Twitter. She plugged her book several times on Twitter, in fact; for example on June 23, 2011, she tweeted: "Finished recording audiobook of my memoir, *Happy Accidents*. 9 hours of me, me, me. Oy."[100]

Validation and a Glimpse into the Future

With more than 150 film and TV credits and a successful autobiography to her name, Lynch has received numerous accolades over the years, most notably her Emmy Award and

Lynch attends a book-signing event for her autobiography,
Happy Accidents, *in 2012. Lynch cowrote the book with*
Lara Embry.

Golden Globe Award for *Glee*. In 2010 she was paid an honor
that has become something of a rite of passage for many well-
known celebrities: She was immortalized in wax by Madame
Tussauds wax museum in Hollywood. Lynch effused at the
unveiling ceremony, "Unbelievable! Oh my God, this is too

much. It's too weird. I feel like I'm seeing myself in a coffin or something."[101]

In 2012 Lynch received another form of recognition for her work when she was awarded an honorary doctorate in fine arts from Smith College, a prestigious, private, liberal women's college in Massachusetts. She also gave the commencement address at the college's graduation ceremonies that spring. During her speech,

Lynch delivers the commencement address at Smith College in Massachusetts after being awarded an honorary doctorate in 2012.

she showed her usual self-effacing humor when she said, "My fellow honorary degree recipients, who I am so proud to be in the company of—we have an architect, a climate scientist, a writer—and I get to talk because I'm on *Glee*. What a world we live in."[102]

Lynch's career continued to grow in 2013. She made her Broadway debut in May playing the less-than-kind orphanage owner Miss Hannigan in the revival of *Annie*, and completed a successful eight-week run in the role. Over that summer Lynch hosted the TV program *Hollywood Game Night*, a show in which Hollywood celebrities are paired with noncelebrity contestants to help them win twenty-five thousand dollars by playing various games. On a personal note, in June 2013 Lynch made the surprising announcement that she and Embry were divorcing after three years of marriage. Lynch filed for divorce, citing irreconcilable differences, in July of that year. Claiming the split was amicable, Lynch explained, "It's just two people who just decide it's better to go apart than stay together."[103]

Lynch's career continues to be robust. Now that she has become successful and well known, however, she no longer has to take any part she can get. "I don't take parts just to do them anymore,"[104] she says. She has come a long way from her childhood days spent watching TV and daydreaming of being on the *Brady Bunch* and *The Mary Tyler Moore Show*. Now that she can be pickier about the parts she chooses, Lynch says she would love to play Greta Garbo, a Hollywood legend from the 1920s and 1930s whom Lynch has idolized for years. She would also love the chance to work with some of her favorite actresses, including Cate Blanchett and Jennifer Saunders.

Although Lynch is now openly gay in real life, she is fine with the fact that her character on *Glee* is not. "I want to be an actor more than I want to be a 'gay actor,'" she says. "I don't just play gay people," she adds, but stresses that she has always been eager to do so. In fact, Lynch wishes there were more gay characters portrayed in movies and on TV. But she remains hopeful and positive about that happening in the future. "History tells us we ultimately weave everyone into the fabric of society," she says. "I think it's just a matter of time."[105]

8 Showcases California's Same-Sex Marriage Issues

In November 2008 California voters approved Proposition 8, a law that banned same-sex marriage by declaring that the state would only recognize marriage between a man and a woman. The law came about in response to the June 2008 legalization of gay marriage in California. Following the vote, a storm of protests erupted throughout California and the country, and a number of lawsuits challenged the legality of the law. Among them was *Perry v. Schwarzenegger*, which was the inspiration for a play by Oscar-winning screenwriter and gay rights activist Dustin Lance Black. The play, aptly called *8*, introduced viewers to the real-life issues and players: the gay and lesbian couples who filed the lawsuit, the attorneys who argued their cases, and the witness who spoke out against them.

The play premiered in March 2012 in Los Angeles and included a star-studded cast. George Clooney and Martin Sheen played cocounsel for the plaintiffs, while Jamie Lee Curtis and Christine Lahti appeared as the lesbian couple who filed the suit. Brad Pitt played the judge, and Kevin Bacon the lead attorney for the Proposition 8 defense team. Another star was Jane Lynch, whose character, a same-sex marriage opponent, could not have been more different from herself. A *Los Angeles Times* review of the play explains: "Lynch enlivened things with her usual wicked wit as Maggie Gallagher, a rabid opponent of same-sex marriage with a bullying style to rival a certain track-suit-wearing toughie on 'Glee.'"

The judge who heard *Perry v. Schwarzenegger* ruled that Proposition 8 was indeed unconstitutional, but after several appeals in the Ninth Circuit Court and the California Supreme Court, the case was brought before the U.S. Supreme Court. In June 2013, the U.S. Supreme Court found that the private parties who put Proposition 8 on the California ballot did not have standing to defend the law in federal courts, making same-sex marriages once again legal in California.

Charles McNulty. "Hollywood Embraces Dustin Lance Black's Prop. 8 Drama." *Culture Monster* (blog), *Los Angeles Times*, March 5, 2012. http://latimesblogs.latimes.com/culturemonster/2012/03/hollywood-embraces-dustin-lance-blacks-prop-8-drama-.html.

Lynch would like to try her hand at directing someday, so perhaps she will get the chance to be a part of bringing more gay characters into mainstream TV and movies. For now, though, she is happy being an actress, because it is what she loves doing. She says that when *Glee* and Sue Sylvester inevitably become old news, she will continue doing what she has done for so many decades. She says, "There was really no choice for me, I have to [act]—this is what I love. And when all of this hype starts to fade, and it will, I will continue."[106]

Introduction: Jane's World

1. Quoted in Camille Mann. "Jane Lynch Launches Website to Educate Students About College Debt." Video. CBS News .com, July 17, 2012. www.cbsnews.com/8301-31749_162 -57474110-10391698/jane-lynch-launches-website-to -educate-students-about-college-debt.
2. Quoted in Mandi Bierly. "Jane Lynch Unveils Wax Sue Sylvester at Madame Tussauds. Watch!" Video. *PopWatch* (blog), EW.com, August 5, 2010. http://popwatch.ew .com/2010/08/05/jane-lynch-madame-tussauds-sue -sylvester.
3. Jane Lynch. *68th Annual Golden Globe Awards*. NBC, January 16, 2011.
4. Hadley Freeman. "Jane Lynch: 'I Came Wired with Extra Angst.'" *Guardian* (Manchester, UK), September 19, 2011. www.guardian.co.uk/culture/2011/sep/19/jane-lynch -emmy-awards-glee?intcmp=239.
5. Quoted in Margy Rochlin. "Jane Lynch's Year of Living Famously." *More*, November 2010. www.more.com/news /womens-issues/jane-lynchs-year-living-famously.
6. Quoted in Freeman. "Jane Lynch: 'I Came Wired with Extra Angst.'"

Chapter 1: A Desire to Be "Normal"

7. Jane Lynch. *Happy Accidents*. New York: Hyperion, 2011, p. 5.
8. Lynch. *Happy Accidents*, p. 7.
9. Quoted in Bill Keveney. "Jane Lynch Shares 'Happy Accidents' of Life." *USA Today*, September 12, 2011. http://usa today30.usatoday.com/life/people/story/2011-09-12/jane -lynch-happy-accidents/50376576/1.
10. Quoted in Ilyssa Panitz. "Jane Lynch, Glee-fully Happy." *More*, September 2011. www.more.com/glee-jane-lynch.

11. Quoted in Andrew Goldman. "See Jane Run." *Elle*, January 24, 2011. www.elle.com/pop-culture/celebrities/jane-lynch.
12. Lynch. *Happy Accidents*, p. 23.
13. Quoted in Keveney. "Jane Lynch Shares 'Happy Accidents' of Life."
14. Quoted in *Morning Edition*. "Jane Lynch: A Life of 'Happy Accidents.'" Video. NPR, September 16, 2011. www.npr.org/player/v2/mediaPlayer.html?action=1&t=1&islist=false&id=140502205&m=140527476.
15. Quoted in Rochlin. "Jane Lynch's Year of Living Famously."
16. Quoted in Dave Itzkoff. "Jane Lynch Brings Her Inner Mean Girl to 'Glee.'" *Arts Beat* (blog), NYTimes.com, May 18, 2009. http://artsbeat.blogs.nytimes.com/2009/05/18/jane-lynch-brings-her-inner-mean-girl-to-glee.
17. Quoted in Panitz. "Jane Lynch, Glee-fully Happy."
18. Quoted in Hamish Bowles. "Queen Jane Lynch." *Vogue*, July 14, 2011. www.vogue.com/magazine/article/queen-jane-lynch/#1.
19. Quoted in Panitz. "Jane Lynch, Glee-fully Happy."
20. Quoted in Bowles. "Queen Jane Lynch."
21. Quoted in David Greene. "Jane Lynch: A Life of 'Happy Accidents.'" Transcript. NPR, September 16, 2011. www.npr.org/templates/transcript/transcript.php?storyId=140502205.
22. It Gets Better Project: Jane Lynch and Lara Embry. www.itgetsbetter.org/video/entry/2574.
23. Quoted in Diane Anderson-Minshall. "Jane Lynch and the Mommy Track (Suit)." *Advocate*, September 12, 2011. www.advocate.com/arts-entertainment/television/2011/09/12/jane-lynch-and-mommy-track-suit.
24. Lynch. *Happy Accidents*, p. 39.
25. Lynch. *Happy Accidents*, p. 48.
26. Lynch. *Happy Accidents*, p. 50.

Chapter 2: The Real Live Jane Lynch

27. Quoted in James Lipton. "Inside the Actors Studio: Cast of *Glee*." Bravo, April 9, 2012. www.youtube.com/watch?v=xyfCHFy8r-k.

28. Lynch. *Happy Accidents*, p. 61.
29. Quoted in Goldman. "See Jane Run."
30. Lynch. *Happy Accidents*, p. 76.
31. Lynch. *Happy Accidents*, p. 80.
32. Quoted in Lipton. "Inside the Actors Studio."
33. Quoted in Goldman. "See Jane Run."
34. Lynch. *Happy Accidents*, p. 90.
35. Quoted in Her Name Is Jane Lynch. "Jane Lynch's Panel at Outfest—Now with Video," July 12, 2010. www.hername isjanelynch.com/2010/07/12/jane-lynchs-panel-at-outfest -now-with-video.
36. Lynch. *Happy Accidents*, p. 101.

Chapter 3: Jobbing Jane

37. Quoted in Danielle Berrin. "Jane Lynch: 'I'm Just a Goof.'" *Guardian* (Manchester, UK), January 8, 2010. www .guardian.co.uk/tv-and-radio/2010/jan/09/jane-lynch -glee-interview.
38. Quoted in Goldman. "See Jane Run."
39. Quoted in Shana Naomi Krochmal. "Out100: Jane Lynch." *Out*, November 15, 2012. www.out.com/out-exclusives /out100-2012/2012/11/15/out100-jane-lynch.
40. Lynch. *Happy Accidents*, p. 136.
41. Quoted in Berrin. "Jane Lynch."
42. Quoted in Goldman. "See Jane Run."
43. Lynch. *Happy Accidents*, pp. 161–162.
44. Quoted in Berrin. "Jane Lynch."
45. Quoted in Rebecca Murray. "Jane Lynch Hits on 'The 40 Year Old Virgin.'" About.com. http://movies.about.com /od/the40yearoldvirgin/a/virginjl081105.htm.
46. Quoted in NPR. "The Many Roles of 'Glee' Meanie Jane Lynch." Audio clip. November 4, 2009. www.npr.org/tem plates/story/story.php?storyId=120086244.
47. Roger Ebert. "*The 40-Year-Old Virgin.*" RogerEbert.com, August 19, 2005. http://rogerebert.suntimes.com/apps/pbcs .dll/article?AID=/20050818/REVIEWS/50803002/1023
48. Total Film. "*Talladega Nights: The Ballad of Ricky Bobby,*" September 15, 2006. www.totalfilm.com/reviews/cinema /talladega-nights-the-ballad-of-ricky-bobby.

49. Lynch. *Happy Accidents*, p. 225.

50. Rick Duran. "*Role Models*—Jane Lynch Interview." Frat Pack Tribute, November 13, 2008. www.the-frat-pack .com/reviews/rolemodels-lynch.html.

51. Quoted in Rochlin. "Jane Lynch's Year of Living Famously."

52. *Julie & Julia*. Directed by Nora Ephron. DVD commentary. Culver City, CA: Columbia Pictures, 2009.

53. Lynch. *Happy Accidents*, p. 231.

54. Michael Slezak. "Jane Lynch: How 'Bout an Oscar Nod for Her Work in 'Julie & Julia'?" *PopWatch* (blog), EW.com, August 14, 2009. http://popwatch.ew.com/2009/08/14 /jane-lynch-julie-julia-oscar.

55. Quoted in Rochlin. "Jane Lynch's Year of Living Famously."

56. Quoted in Patti Greco. "Jane Lynch's Little Secret." *More*, November 2010. www.more.com/news/womens-issues /jane-lynchs-little-secret.

57. Quoted in *Fox All Access*. "Jane Lynch: Charlie Sheen Is One of the Nicest Guys in the World." Audio clip. http://fox allaccess.blogs.fox.com/2011/08/05/jane-lynch-charlie -sheen-is-one-of-the-nicest-guys-in-the-world.

58. Allison Glock. "She Likes to Watch." *New York Times*, February 6, 2005. www.nytimes.com/2005/02/06/arts /television/06gloc.html?pagewanted=all.

59. Quoted in Andrew Goldman. "See Jane Run."

60. Quoted in Itzkoff. "Jane Lynch Brings Her Inner Mean Girl to 'Glee.'"

61. *Glee*. Season 1, episode 18. Fox, May 11, 2010.

62. Lisa Respers France. "Some of the Best of 2009's TV." CNN Entertainment, December 23, 2009. www.cnn.com/2009 /SHOWBIZ/TV/12/23/best.tv.2009/index.html.

63. Kelly Cogswell. "See Jane Lynch Run." *The Blog, Huffington Post*, October 12, 2011. www.huffingtonpost.com/kelly -cogswell/see-jane-lynch-run_b_981151.html.

64. Goldman. "See Jane Run."

65. Quoted in Judith Newman. "Jane Lynch Finds Herself." *New York Times*, September 16, 2011. www.nytimes .com/2011/09/18/fashion/jane-lynch-finds-herself.html ?pagewanted=all&_r=0.

Chapter 4: A Late Bloomer

66. Quoted in Panitz. "Jane Lynch, Glee-fully Happy."
67. Quoted in Panitz. "Jane Lynch, Glee-fully Happy."
68. Lynch. *Happy Accidents*, p. 107.
69. Quoted in Crystal G. Martin. "Jane Lynch's Aha! Moment." *Oprah Magazine*, June 2010. www.oprah.com/spirit/Glees-Jane-Lynch-on-When-Its-Not-About-You.
70. Quoted in Greene. "Jane Lynch: A Life of '*Happy Accidents*.'"
71. Lynch. *Happy Accidents*, p. 124.
72. Quoted in Linda Rapp. "Lynch, Jane." glbtq, 2006. www.glbtq.com/arts/lynch_j.html.
73. Quoted in Jessica Bennett. "Dan Savage and Jane Lynch." Daily Beast, December 20, 2010. www.thedailybeast.com/newsweek/2010/12/20/dan-savage-and-jane-lynch.html.
74. *The Ellen DeGeneres Show*. NBC, September 15, 2010. www.celebuzz.com/jane-lynch-talks-coming-out-s251011.
75. *The Ellen DeGeneres Show*.
76. Lynch. *Happy Accidents*, p. 177.
77. Lynch. *Happy Accidents*, p. 182
78. Lynch. *Happy Accidents*, p. 108.
79. Lynch. *Happy Accidents*, p. 3.
80. Quoted in Paula Schwartz. "Jane Lynch and Lara Embry." *New York Times*, June 2, 2010. www.nytimes.com/2010/06/06/fashion/weddings/06JLYNCH.html?_r=0.
81. Quoted in Bowles. "Queen Jane Lynch."
82. Quoted in Bowles. "Queen Jane Lynch."
83. Quoted in Schwartz. "Jane Lynch and Lara Embry."
84. Quoted in Greene. "Jane Lynch."

Chapter 5: Activist Jane

85. Quoted in Rebecca Nicholson. "Emmys 2011: Host Jane Lynch on *Glee*, Projectile Vomiting and Homophobia." *Guardian* (Manchester, UK), September 17, 2011. www.guardian.co.uk/culture/2011/sep/18/jane-lynch-glee-emmy-awards-emmys.
86. It Gets Better Project: Jane Lynch and Lara Embry.
87. Quoted in Her Name Is Jane Lynch. "Jane Lynch's Panel at Outfest."

88. Quoted in Access Hollywood. "'Glee' Stars 'Touched' by Pitt & Clooney's Support of '8,'" March 5, 2012. www.ac cesshollywood.com/glee-stars-touched-by-brad-pitt-and -george-clooneys-support-of-8_article_61543.
89. Jane Lynch. Twitter. June 25, 2011. https://twitter.com /janemarielynch.
90. Quoted in Lucas Grindley. "See Why Jane Lynch Is Boycot-ting Amway." *Advocate*, October 11, 2012. www.advocate .com/business/2012/10/11/see-why-jane-lynch-boycot ting-amway.
91. Michelle Kretzer. "Jane Lynch Not 'Glee'ful About Aquarium Party." *PETA Files* (blog), PETA, September 14, 2012. www.peta.org/b/thepetafiles/archive/2012/09/14 /jane-lynch-not-glee-ful-about-atlanta-pride-aquarium -party.aspx.
92. Jane Lynch. "LG Text Ed with Jane Lynch." Video. www .lg.com/us/mobile-phones/text-education/jane-lynch.jsp.
93. Jane Lynch. Twitter. August 6, 2011. https://twitter.com /janemarielynch.
94. Quoted in Camille Mann. "Jane Lynch Launches Website to Educate Students About College Debt."
95. Quoted in Shana Naomi Krochmal. "Out100: Jane Lynch."
96. Quoted in Bowles. "Queen Jane Lynch."
97. Bowles. "Queen Jane Lynch."
98. Quoted in Keveney. "Jane Lynch Shares 'Happy Accidents' of Life."
99. Jane Lynch. Twitter. September 13, 2011. https://twitter .com/janemarielynch.
100. Jane Lynch. Twitter. June 23, 2011. https://twitter.com /janemarielynch.
101. Quoted in Bierly. "Jane Lynch Unveils Wax Sue Sylvester at Madame Tussauds.
102. Quoted in Hawckward. "Jane Lynch Delivers Commence-ment Address to the Class of 2012." Video. *Smith'd* (blog), May 20, 2012. http://smithd.org/2012/05/20/watch-jane -lynch-delivers-commencement-address-to-the-class -of-2012.

103. CBSNews.com. "Jane Lynch Opens Up About Her Divorce." July 16, 2013. www.cbsnews.com/8301-207_162 -57594007/jane-lynch-opens-up-about-her-divorce.

104. Quoted in Bowles. "Queen Jane Lynch."

105. Quoted in Rapp. "Lynch, Jane."

106. Quoted in Her Name Is Jane Lynch. "Jane Lynch's Panel at Outfest."

1960

Jane Marie Lynch is born in Dolton, Illinois, on July 14.

1972

Discovers what "being gay" means and realizes for the first time that she is gay.

1974

Is cast as the king in the school play *The Ugly Duckling* but drops out and is branded a quitter.

1976

Begins drinking beer regularly at age sixteen.

1978

Appears in school production of *Godspell*; graduates from Thornridge High School with a C average; starts college at Illinois State University (ISU) and soon switches her major to the ater arts.

1982

Graduates from ISU with a degree in theater arts.

1984

Graduates from Cornell University with an master of fine arts degree in theater; moves to New York City to pursue a career in acting and winds up taking a desk job at an advertising agency.

1985

Moves back to Chicago and takes a job as a receptionist at the Civic Opera House; lands a part in a William Shakespeare company production of *The Comedy of Errors*.

1987

Takes a gig hawking products on the TV home-shopping show *America's Shopping Place*; auditions for and is cast in The Second City touring company.

1988

Makes her film debut in the box office flop *Vice Versa*.

1990

Is cast by the Steppenwolf Theatre Company in a series of short plays; works with the company off and on for the next ten years; joins the cast of *The Real Live Brady Bunch*.

1991

Decides to quit drinking but continues alcohol addiction by daily use of Nyquil, a liquid cold remedy that contains alcohol.

1992

Joins Alcoholics Anonymous to help her overcome her alcohol dependency; comes out to her parents in a letter.

1993

Appears in the blockbuster film *The Fugitive* with Harrison Ford; moves to Los Angeles.

1998

Writes and performs in stage show *Oh, Sister, My Sister!*, which wins the Best Comedy Ensemble of the Year Award from *LA Weekly*.

2000

Appears in the hit movie *Best in Show*, directed by Christopher Guest; buys her first house, in the Hollywood Hills neighborhood of Laurel Canyon.

2003

Appears in Guest's *A Mighty Wind*, in which she sings and plays the guitar.

2004

Begins a recurring role as a therapist on the hit CBS sitcom *Two and a Half Men*.

2005

Appears in the Judd Apatow comedy *The 40-Year-Old Virgin* starring Steve Carell; lands a recurring role as a feminist lesbian lawyer in fifteen episodes of the Showtime drama *The L Word*; is named one of the 10 Amazing Women in Showbiz by the Professional Organization of Women in Entertainment Reaching Up (POWER UP).

2006

Plays Will Ferrell's mother in *Talladega Nights: The Ballad of Ricky Bobby*.

2008

Appears in the hit comedy *Role Models*.

2009

Meets psychologist Lara Embry and begins a long-distance relationship with her; appears in *Julie & Julia*; is cast as snarky cheerleading coach Sue Sylvester in the new Fox musical comedy, *Glee*.

2010

Marries Embry; is nominated for a Primetime Emmy for her role on *Two and a Half Men*; wins both an Emmy Award and a Golden Globe Award for her role on *Glee*.

2011

Wins Golden Globe Award for her work on *Glee*; her autobiography, *Happy Accidents*, becomes a best seller; hosts the 63rd Primetime Emmy Awards, becoming only the third solo female host in the show's history.

2012

Appears in *The Three Stooges*; appears in the play 8; speaks out publicly against the restaurant chain Chick Fil-A for its stance against same-sex marriage; is named *Out* magazine's Entertainer of the Year; is awarded an honorary doctorate in fine arts from Smith College.

2013

Makes Broadway debut as Miss Hannigan in *Annie*, a role Lynch's idol Carol Burnett played in the 1982 feature film adaptation; announces and files for divorce from Embry; hosts the TV show *Hollywood Game Night*.

For More Information

Books

Jane Lynch. *Happy Accidents*. New York: Voice/Hyperion, 2012. In this autobiography, Lynch offers readers a chance to get to know her as a person, and see how hard she has worked to achieve her dream of being an actress—and to accept herself for who she is rather than who others might expect her to be.

Debra Mostow Zakarin and the creators of *Glee*. *Glee: The Official William McKinley High School Yearbook*. New York: Poppy, 2012. This "yearbook" of the fictional high school featured on the hit musical comedy-drama contains numerous full-color photographs of many of the principal characters on *Glee*.

Periodicals

Joshua Alston. "Laughably Larcenous." *Newsweek*, September 7, 2009.

Matthew Belloni and Stacey Wilson. "Free Association with TV's Funny Ladies." *Hollywood Reporter*, June 29, 2012.

Jessica Bennett. "Dan Savage and Jane Lynch." *Newsweek*, January 3, 2011.

Kevin Fallon. "How Jane Lynch Went from Wannabe Actress to Emmys Host." *Atlantic*, September 2011.

Laura Fitzpatrick. "Jane Lynch Best in Show." *Time*, April 26, 2010.

Byron Katie and Jane Lynch. "Ready to Get to Work? Bring It On!" *Los Angeles Magazine*, October 2011.

Shana Naomi Krochmal. "Out100: Jane Lynch." *Out*, November 15, 2012.

David Kronke. "Her 'Hero's Journey' to Host Gig." *Daily Variety*, August 22, 2011.

Sarah Kuhn. "Cheers to Her." *Backstage*, June 3, 2010.

Julie Naughton. "Jane Lynch to Make Her Beauty Industry Debut." *WWD*, May 18, 2012.

Judith Newman. "Jane Lynch Finds Herself." *New York Times*, September 16, 2011.

Edie Stull. "Accidentally Fabulous." *Curve*, December 2011.

George Wayne. "Not Your Average Jane." *Vanity Fair*, October 2011.

Internet Sources

Hamish Bowles. "Queen Jane Lynch." *Vogue*, July 14, 2011. www.vogue.com/magazine/article/queen-jane-lynch/#1.

J.D. Cargill. "'Glee's' Jane Lynch Moves from Screen to Page." CNN, December 12, 2012. www.cnn.com/2012/12/07/show biz/celebrity-news-gossip/jane-lynch-elfbot/index.html.

Caitlin Colford. "Jane Lynch's Got Game, and More, as Tough Sergeant in New Animated Film 'Wreck-It Ralph,'" *New York Daily News*, October 29, 2012. www.nydailynews.com/enter tainment/tv-movies/jane-lynch-enlists-sgt-calhoun-wreck-it -ralph-article-1.1193349.

Robert DeSalvo. "Q&A: Jane Lynch on Being the Toughest Video Game Vixen in 'Wreck-It Ralph.'" *Next Movie Blog.* Next Movie, November 2, 2012. www.nextmovie.com/blog/jane-lynch-wreck-it-ralph-interview.

Emmys.com. "Share: All About Jane," September 14, 2011. www.emmys.com/articles/share-all-about-jane-0.

Alexandra Galkin. "'Glee' Star Jane Lynch Wanted to Be Con-sidered 'Normal' Growing Up: 'I Didn't Want to Be Gay." *New York Daily News*, July 16, 2011. www.nydailynews.com/en tertainment/gossip/glee-star-jane-lynch-wanted-considered -normal-growing-didn-gay-article-1.158862.

Lucas Grindley. "See Why Jane Lynch Is Boycotting Amway." *Advocate*, October 11, 2012. www.advocate.com/business /2012/10/11/see-why-jane-lynch-boycotting-amway.

Jim Hill. "Jane Lynch on How She Almost *Wreck-It Ralph*-ed Her Career." *Huffington Post*, November 2, 2012. www.huffing tonpost.com/jim-hill/jane-lynch-wreck-it-ralph_b_2059789 .html.

Dave Itzkoff. "Jane Lynch Brings Her Inner Mean Girl to 'Glee,'" *Arts Beat* (blog). NYTimes.com, May 18, 2009. http://artsbeat .blogs.nytimes.com/2009/05/18/jane-lynch-brings-her-inner -mean-girl-to-glee.

Zach Johnson. "Jane Lynch: My Stepdaughter Is 'Not at All in Awe' of My Acting Fame." *Us Weekly*, January 11, 2013. www .usmagazine.com/celebrity-moms/news/jane-lynch-my-step daughter-is-not-at-all-in-awe-of-my-acting-fame-2013111.

Michelle Kretzer. "Jane Lynch Not 'Glee'ful About Aquarium Party." PETA Files, September 14, 2012. www.peta.org/b /thepetafiles/archive/2012/09/14/jane-lynch-not-glee-ful -about-atlanta-pride-aquarium-party.aspx.

Camille Mann. "Jane Lynch Launches Website to Educate Students About College Debt." CBS News, July 17, 2012. www .cbsnews.com/8301-31749_162-57474110-10391698/jane -lynch-launches-website-to-educate-students-about-college -debt.

Brian Stewart. "Jane Lynch: 'Younger Generations Have Always Been Progressive,'" August 8, 2012. http://campusprogress .org/articles/jane_lynch_younger_generations_have_always _been_progressive.

Websites

Epic School Battle, Adopt the Arts (http://adoptthearts.org /epic-school-battle-psa). The mission of the Adopt the Arts Foundation is to bring together entertainers, public figures, and the general public to save the arts in America's public schools. This site contains information about and a link to the public service announcement (PSA) featuring Jane Lynch.

Her Name Is Jane Lynch (www.hernameisjanelynch.com). This fan site will delight visitors with its collection of news articles, interviews, and special sections titled *Glee* and *Not Glee*. It also contains a clip of Lynch performing onstage in *The Real Live Brady Bunch*.

It Gets Better Project: Jane Lynch and Lara Embry (www .itgetsbetter.org/video/entry/2574). This is the video made by Lynch and Embry in support of the It Gets Better Project, which offers support to lesbian, gay, bisexual, and transgender youth.

Jane Lynch Fan Club (www.fanpop.com/clubs/jane-lynch). This site includes everything Lynch fans could possibly want, including articles, videos, a huge collection of photos, a discussion forum, and links to other sites.

Steppenwolf Theatre Company (www.steppenwolf.org). Lynch was once part of this renowned, award-winning theater troupe in Chicago.

Picture Credits

About the Author

Cherese Cartlidge holds a bachelor's degree in psychology and a master's degree in education. She is the author of more than twenty books for children and young adults, including biographies of Prince Harry, Taylor Swift, Neil Patrick Harris, and Anne Hathaway. Cartlidge lives in Georgia with her two children.